THE DING-DONG ALTAR BOY

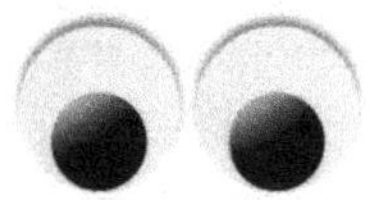

AND OTHER TALES OF AN AFFIRMATION JUNKIE

BY DONALD OSBORN
AND
ANNA HENKENS SCHMIDT

This is a work of nonfiction. The stories contained herein are based on true events and lived experience, filtered through memory, time, and the occasional emotional exaggeration. Names and identifying details may have been changed to protect privacy—or because the author genuinely couldn't remember them. Any resemblance to actual people is most likely intentional and hopefully flattering. If not, a sincere apology and a beer will be considered upon request.

Legal & Safety Notice (you know, just in case):

Nothing in this book should be considered medical, legal, nutritional, psychological, or life-coaching advice. Any attempts to replicate the author's decisions—culinary, romantic, or otherwise—are undertaken at your own risk. The author is not responsible for stubbed toes, awkward conversations, or sudden urges to move back to your hometown.

Permissions: You are warmly encouraged to laugh, reminisce, cry a little, and share the funny bits with people who knew you when. You are not permitted to fact-check the author (memory is fragile), file grievances with past versions of people, or try to turn any part of this book into a self-help seminar. Proceed with curiosity, kindness, and a grain of salt.

Edited by Brianna Rowe.

First paperback edition July 2025
ISBN-979-8-9902833-4-3 (paperback)
www.annahenkenschmidt.com

To everyone who has ever called Chadron,

Nebraska, home — with special affection for

the Chadron High School Class of 1975.

THE DING-DONG ALTAR BOY PLAYLIST

This book comes with a carefully curated Spotify playlist handpicked by Donald to accompany each story. Two original songs by the author are featured, "Drunk on Wine," and "Kenny in the Tree." Scan the QR code to listen, or check the Table of Contents for a full song-by-story guide.

Table of Contents and Playlist

NOTE FROM THE COAUTHOR, ANNA HENKENS SCHMIDT

For unknown reasons, I had an obsession with Elvis Presley in third grade.

At one point there was recorded evidence on VHS of me performing a dance routine to "Jailhouse Rock" in my basement, complete with a wooden chair. To the best of my knowledge, this video was thrown out or destroyed.

Please God, may it be so.

I knew every lyric to "Blue Suede Shoes" and "Love Me Tender." I'd fall asleep to cassette tapes of "All Shook Up" and imagine Elvis appearing on my doorstep proposing marriage. Of course, my childhood fantasies couldn't comprehend our 44-year age gap, or the fact he'd already overdosed two years before my birth.

Then again, Elvis dated Priscilla when she was just 14, so who knows? Maybe a nine-year-old fan wouldn't have been off his radar.

When I was admitted into the Talented and Gifted (TAG) program at Eastward Elementary School in Chadron, Nebraska, the teachers were quick to sense their mistake. While the other kids were writing research papers about flamingos and dolphins, I was checking out books about Elvis Presley and writing about his singing career as well as the barbiturates and amphetamines that led to his death.

Some might have called me a strange child.

And I was.

But I was also born into a strange family.

Some parents may have monitored their children's reading habits, or gently suggested I stop trying to figure out exactly how many times Elvis cheated on his wife, but my parents left me on a long leash. I don't mean 'leash' metaphorically. I also used to pretend I was a dog far longer than was age appropriate, but really, haven't I embarrassed myself enough already? And this isn't even my book.

Which brings me to my oldest brother, Donald.

How can I possibly transition from discussing the King of Rock and Roll to discussing my brother?

Easy. The two are forever linked in my mind.

Discovering my bizarre Elvis fixation, Donald decided it was the perfect opportunity to give me the inside scoop on our family. "Hey, I knew Elvis," he said.

"Really?"

"Oh yeah. He was our uncle."

"He was?"

Let it be noted I didn't have a strong grasp on

genealogy. Nowhere in my 9-year-old brain did it register that if Elvis was indeed my mother's brother, I'd have heard of it long ago.

"Would I lie to you?" Donald asked me.

I nodded my head.

"Well, this is true," he said. "Ask Mom."

"MMMMOOOOO—"

He put a hand over my mouth. "Don't ask Mom. She's busy. Anyway, we called him Uncle Elvis. Sometimes he'd play songs for us on his guitar, and I said, 'Hey Elvis, I have this great idea. How about a song called Hound Dog?'"

"That's a lie."

"No it's not. How else would he have come up with that?"

I shrugged.

Donald continued to spin bigger and more elaborate tales of his memories of Uncle Elvis. I sat, enraptured, asking more and more questions, sure I could catch Donald in a contradiction. I walked away believing without a doubt that one thing was absolutely true. My brother was a storyteller.

I never once believed Elvis was my uncle. However, that in no way stopped me from marching into school and bragging about my famous family connection. I kept this story alive for years, despite the fact no one cared. My friends might have perked up their ears for New Kids on the Block or Madonna, but not some dead guy who never gave up the dream of the white jumpsuit despite being 180 pounds overweight.

But I didn't really care what the other kids thought.

They could have their flamingos and dolphins.

Real or imagined, I was more drawn to stories.

Donald was the purveyor of my earliest stories. He convinced me he could actually steal the nose off my face and hold it painlessly in the palm of his hand. Eventually, I began to dodge out of his arm's reach, wary that this time he might not return my nose and I'd have yet another thing setting me apart from my peers.

He had a knack for making up songs for every occasion, endlessly serenading me with "Anna Mario Hinko Stinko" in a melody I'll never forget.

Donald also introduced me to Nap-Nap Monster, a game where he'd lie on the couch pretending to nap while I tiptoed closer and closer, caught between the thrill and the fear of being captured. Only later did I realize this was a low-effort strategy to entertain me with minimal exertion on his part.

It's a brilliant invention I've since passed down to my own children.

Donald's storytelling prowess, from Elvis fabrications to couch monster games, was always part of my world—and it was only a matter of time before it led to something bigger.

When Donald first approached me with the concept that was to become our first book, *Where We Land: A Pilot's Reflections at Altitude*, I had my doubts. There wasn't a lot of wiggle room in my schedule. How would I have time to write a book?

But the stories drew me in.

Of course I'd heard many of them before—and I'd heard them many, many times—but, other stories were new to me. As I compiled these stories and essays and turned them into chapters, and as the chapters turned into a book, it was as if an artist layered paints until a portrait emerged. Though I'd known my brother my entire life, it took writing a book together before I really saw Donald and all the struggles he'd faced.

Still, there is far more to a person than can fit between 209 paperback pages.

After the publication of *Where We Land*, the flood of feedback began. While most of the comments were complimentary, Donald heard the same questions over and over again.

"Why didn't you write about that one time . . ."

"Oh, thank God you didn't write about that one time . . ."

"I can't wait for the sequel!"

Often these stories were not airplane related and didn't fit the theme of *Where We Land*, a memoir and commentary on the airline industry. "It's a good story," I'd say, "but it has nothing to do with this book."

So just as I thought my ghost-writing days were through, Donald contacted me again.

"What if we did a book of short stories?"

"Um."

"We can write all the stories that didn't fit in the first book."

"I don't know. Maybe," I said, as noncommittally as

possible.

More than a year has passed since that conversation, and you are holding the evidence of my decision in your hand.

This book is a little different from our first one. Each chapter stands alone as a complete story or essay. It's more like a series of short flights than a cross-country journey.

Donald brought the stories, and I shaped them into something readable. The result? His stories, my words. Simple as that. Donald's voice is still the backbone of every tale. My job was to make the stories work on paper, smooth out the rough edges, and make sure it all came together without losing what makes it his.

Whether you're here for the belly laughs, the heartfelt moments, or the occasional tale of familial chaos, this book has something for everyone.

As a bonus, this book comes with its own soundtrack, carefully curated by Donald. Music has always been a huge part of his life, and he's picked out the perfect songs to go along with each story. In fact, two of the tracks are ones he's written himself. So be sure to check out the Table of Contents, where you'll find a curated list of songs to complement each story, along with a link to the Spotify playlist. It's a perfect soundtrack to this collection of tales.

Unlike the Elvis tales of my childhood, everything in this book is true—sometimes hilariously, sometimes heartbreakingly. But Donald's magic lies in the way he tells a story, whether it's about flying planes or pretending to nap on the couch. And maybe that's what I'll always admire most about him: his ability to turn life into stories, and his insistence that every one of them was worth telling.

RED INK AND
RUN-ON DREAMS

Finally, a school assignment that excited me.

I took out my pencil.

The next thing I knew the wind smacked against my face, carrying the woodsy scent of pine trees, sunbaked asphalt, and metallic exhaust fumes. The tires of my 1952 Harley-Davidson Hydra-Glide chewed the blackened concrete as the world rushed by. My friends and I were on a trip of a lifetime. We stopped to refuel, eat, and sleep, but mostly we just ran the motors on our choppers until we saw every last wonder of the present-day American world. The Statue of Liberty, Disney World, The Grand Canyon, and The Golden Gate Bridge flashed in our periphery. We lived off the land and our exuberant youthfulness.

"Donald, this is not a nice story."

The paper landed on my desk with a disappointed crinkle. Sister Monica glared down at me, pointing her finger at the red letter D at the top of the page. Misspellings, run-on sentences, and punctuation mistakes were circled in the same red ink. My story was a murder victim. Sister Monica dangled my participles to death. Every misplaced modifier lay bleeding in the margins.

I gulped.

"Not only were your punctuation choices regrettable, but riding a motorcycle across the country with your friends is hardly an aspiration worth pursuing."

I nodded, not daring to lift my eyes away from my paper.

I'd always been drawn to storytelling, and I'd gotten such a thrill seeing my story unfold in my notebook. Sure, I'd apparently switched between present and past-tense verbs a few times, but I'd stayed in character. On the whole, it was a pretty impressive story for a fourth grader. But Sister Monica couldn't see beyond my forgetfulness to use capital letters at the beginnings of sentences, nor could she embrace the imagination of a little boy. They say the pen is mightier than the sword. I agree. With her red pen, Sister Monica slashed any hopes I had to become a writer.

Thankfully grammar was not a prerequisite in the airline industry. I soared to great heights in my career without ever knowing the definition of a nominative pronoun. On a few occasions, I even submitted articles to ALPA (Air Lines Pilot Association) Magazine and was published. A picture of President Obama and me was printed in the national edition after I flew him around during the 2008 presidential campaign. In that same magazine, there's a picture of me on page 6, next to an article I wrote about my new position on the Master Executive Council. Writing for ALPA was easy, because it was a niche audience. Also, I've known a lot of pilots in my life, and not one of them could point out a nominative pronoun, so no one came running after me with red pens.

Still, it was nice to see my name in print. I considered mailing a copy to Sister Monica. Thankfully, as a mature adult, I was no longer hung up on the injustices committed against my 10-year-old self. Also, she was probably dead.

As I progressed through my flying career, the idea of writing a book kept circling through my mind. Flying gave me an entirely new perspective—on the world below, yes, but also on the stories I wanted to tell. There was much more to the airline industry than the average passenger knew. I wanted to write an exposé detailing what goes on behind the scenes and expose the dirty underbelly unknown to the flying public. I even had a title—*Flying Sausage*. The idea behind the title was simple. People like to eat sausage, but they don't necessarily want to know how it's made. The same can be said for flying. It's one thing to be a passenger and quite another to be a pilot. The book would focus on the pilot's perspective and explore all the parts about the airline industry that the flying public didn't know.

My wife thought it was a bad idea and a waste of time.

Undeterred, I wrote up a few chapters and sent it to an editor. She returned it with more red marks than Sister Monica and said she didn't see any commercial value to it.

Once again, I put aside my pen.

Perhaps a book was too large an undertaking.

As a music lover, I often found that certain words would get stuck in my head on a loop. They weren't words from other people's songs. Rather these were my own words playing over and over again in my brain. Sometimes I found myself humming melodies that matched the cadence of the sentences. One day it dawned on me. These were song lyrics. Once a song was stuck in my brain, the only way to get it out was to write the lyrics on paper. Soon I had a whole stack of original music.

I'd take the songs and fiddle around with my guitar, strum different chords until it sounded right, and the next thing I knew, a song was born.

I had connections with a recording studio outside of Chicago. Steve Ashum, the leader of Product Recording Company, called me up one day. "We'd like to record *Drunk on Wine*," he said, naming one of the songs I wrote.

"That's great!" I said into the phone. "How cool."

A few weeks later I was in Chicago and stopped by the studio. "Hey," Steve said. "We aren't through with this yet, but have a listen."

He turned up on the volume and there was my song, but way better than I'd imagined it. I'd come up with a simple melody line and lyrics, but the band added guitar, drums, and vocals, all by musicians much more talented than I. When I shared my music with Steve, he hadn't just heard the song. He heard the potential and what the song could become.

I remember looking at Steve, almost teary-eyed. "I'm a

writer, aren't I?"

"Damn right you are," he said.

An artistic creation brings a unique sort of joy when it's born into the world. Whether it's a short story, song lyric, or an article for ALPA Magazine, there is an almost giddy feeling that you've had a chance to bring an inspiration to life.

In the end, the band produced an album almost exclusively from my lyrics. Through the process, I learned an important lesson: creation is not a solo endeavor. It may be true that Jackson Pollock was usually alone when he threw buckets of paint at canvases, but there was no evidence he was happy with his art. He struggled with alcoholism his entire life and crashed into a tree at age 54, dying on impact. I believe a more rich and satisfying form of creation involves collaboration.

I could have played my songs into a cassette recorder and called myself a song writer. But my favorite songs are the product of a whole band, each member showcasing his talents and coming together to make something on a higher level, something a single person couldn't have reached on his own.

Years went by. I flew more planes. I wrote more songs. And still the idea of a book wouldn't go away. But it was a daunting project. I still struggled with capital letters and period placements. I couldn't tell a subject from a predicate. Could I really write a book?

My youngest sibling, Annie, had always been a writer. She had a background in journalism and public relations. She'd even won a few awards back in the day. She hadn't had Sister Monica as a teacher, but if she had, my sneaking suspicions tell me she would have seen a red A at the top of her page.

I called her up one day and told her my book idea. "I want to call it *Flying Sausage*," I said.

"Oh my God, no," she said.

"Why not?"

"Honestly? Because it sounds like a bad penis joke."

"Your mind is in the gutter," I said.

"No. I swear everyone will think that." She pulled the phone away, and I could hear her talking to someone in the background, probably her husband. "I just asked Trevor and he thinks it sounds like a plane full of male strippers."

"What is wrong with your family?" I asked.

"Nothing. It's a terrible name."

"Fine . . . But what do you think? Can we write this thing?"

She laughed. "I've been raising kids for the last 15 years. The only things I've written are the annual Christmas letter and the occasional Facebook status."

"It's like riding a bike."

"You do realize I'm homeschooling three children? When am I going to have time to write a book? Between high school Latin and Kindergarten phonics?"

"That works for me."

I could almost hear her roll her eyes. "Fine. Send me what you've got. I'll take a look."

A week later, she emailed me the first chapter. It was my story, but somehow I was transported back in time by her words. It was as though she'd been there beside me as a 14-year-old kid sneaking into the machine shed to get my first up-close glimpse of an airplane. The words came alive in a way they wouldn't have done for me alone.

I told her how much I liked it.

"You're a natural storyteller," she told me. "You've got all the ideas, the metaphors, and the life experiences. But your run-on sentences have run-on sentences."

Sister Monica would have stopped those runaway sentences with a red pen, but Annie took a different approach. She provided the background music to my lyrics, and the song came to life in a way I hadn't foreseen. Instead of a guitar, she used a pen. Rather than a drum set, she used a word processor. Because she didn't focus on all my mistakes, I had the freedom to be creative.

At the same time, she wasn't afraid to tell me when I was being an idiot. In return, I gave her the freedom to make all the decisions that were in her wheelhouse.

When she told me she wanted to hire our niece, Brianna Rowe, to edit our book, I wondered if it was necessary. Did we really need any more instruments in this band? From my perspective, it sounded pretty good already.

Annie likes to point out that she's right most of the time, and while this is debatable, she was right about hiring an editor. Brianna was a bit ruthless, like Sister Monica with a pen, but she didn't slash through things because she thought they were bad, but because she saw where they could be better. Brianna was the soundboard editor, who brought all the instruments into perfect balance.

Brianna didn't like the *Flying Sausage* title either. I was unanimously outvoted on that one. But she did help us land on the title of our first book.

I remember the first time I held a copy of *Where We Land: A Pilot's Reflections at Altitude*. It was surreal. My name was on the cover. I was a published author. It was better than anything I could have done alone. It was a creative collaboration. The book won awards. We were featured on websites, live TV shows, radio shows, and podcasts. We received favorable reviews.

More importantly, as I held the book in my hands, I was able to reconnect with my inner fourth-grade child. "Hey Donald," I whispered. "You did it. You are a writer."

Suck it, Sister Monica.

DOGGONE WORLD

I walked at nine months. So by the age of one, I decided the time had come to strike out on my own. As the story goes, I was clad only in my diaper, but strode with confidence up the alley that nestled between Shelton and King Street. At the time, we lived on the 100 block of Shelton in our small town of Chadron, Nebraska. Even at that young age, I must have felt a magnetic pull towards Highway 20, somehow sensing that this longest road in the United States Highway System would take me wherever I wanted to go. Only three blocks separated me from escape.

Three measly blocks and a Labrador mix named Blackie.

The sudden disappearance of a diaper-clad one-year-old caused all manner of alarm. While I felt the pull of freedom, Mom felt the pull to keep me alive. She searched the yard frantically, calling my name, and soon the neighbors were out helping her look.

Since my departure wasn't preplanned, I didn't have

luggage or supplies, only that one diaper. But I had good company. The family dog, Blackie, stuck right next to me. I'm sure I appreciated the companionship, but when he heard Mom and the others yelling my name, he barked and gave away our location.

Thanks to that dog, I didn't make my big escape until years later. And looking back, it was probably for the best. Though I don't recollect Blackie personally, I remember seeing his picture. His nobility shone through the faded Polaroid snapshot. Those dark eyes contained wisdom. Though the dog had been lost to time and now only existed on a brown-tinged photograph, I felt like I could still communicate with him.

Blackie was my first canine co-conspirator, but he wouldn't be my last. I can't remember a time when we didn't have at least one dog in the house. Mom naturally attracted dogs, even without trying. If she walked down the street, one of the town strays would find her and beg attention.

I must have inherited Mom's dog-whispering gifts. I swear to God I speak their language. I've been translating dog language since before I could spell my own name. Their thoughts come through clear as day. I've never found such understanding amongst the human race.

One of the first times I didn't own a dog came right after I began my career as a pilot. In those early years, I moved from place to place, chasing the next opportunity to fly. Life wasn't settled enough for a pet. I met my wife, Beth, and she did her best to tame me. We moved to Omaha. While we both wanted a dog, it didn't seem the right time to add to our family. I traveled a lot and we'd just moved into a brand-new home. The idea of a dog coming in and destroying our first big investment didn't appeal to either one of us.

One day we found ourselves in front of a pet store staring at these five little puppies playing in the front window. We reiterated the reasons we couldn't own a dog, repeated them like a mantra, and walked away.

A day later we found ourselves in front of the pet store window a second time. Only one puppy remained, a kind of mutt, likely a mix of terrier, Pekingese, miniature poodle, and schnauzer. His shaggy brownish-blond hair grew over his eyes, and his snout and the tips of ears looked like they'd been dipped in black paint. He resembled Benji, the famous dog from the 1970s movies.

Through the window, he stared at us with sad eyes. His voice penetrated into my innermost being. Now, as I've explained, I speak Dog. It's not a formal language, and I don't teach classes, but someone had to translate. "Oh no!" he said. "Look, they took my brothers!"

Again, Beth and I walked away, reminding ourselves a dog didn't fit into our lifestyle and responsibilities. We were in the midst of chores at home when Beth abruptly grabbed the car keys. "Hey, I've got to go do something," she said. "I'll be right back."

Beth didn't return alone. Tucked in her arms wiggled the cutest dog on the planet. I can't state enough that never before in the history of the world had a more irresistible creature existed.

Unfortunately he knew he could get away with anything. As his first crime, he dug a hole in the new living room carpet. "So what?" he said. "I'm cute." He peed and pooped all over the place. We named him Bandit, because he was a criminal.

We decided Bandit needed a buddy, an older dog who'd teach him to behave. We visited the local Humane Society, and that's where we found Buddy, a poodle-mix so jet black you couldn't see his eyes. Bandit greeted his friend with some suspicion. "Welcome to the rock," he told Buddy. "A few house rules you have to know. My Mommy. My Daddy. My toys. My house."

Buddy settled in easily. Whenever we'd ask Buddy what he was doing, he'd say, "Being good." Buddy, the tolerant older brother, looked at Bandit and sighed, because the younger dog found trouble wherever he went. The dogs had distinct temperaments. Bandit was like the pretty cheerleader who got by on looks, and Buddy was the less attractive side-kick who relied on his personality. Buddy remained docile and sweet-natured, unless a person needed biting. Come to think of it, Buddy bit quite a few people over his lifetime. Goes to show how smart dogs are. I can think of plenty of people who need a good chomp, but I've learned that among the human species, biting others is not socially accepted. Another good reason to have a dog.

Bandit and Buddy were with us through every move. When the airline I worked for went out of business, we could no longer afford our nice house in Omaha, so we moved to an old beat-up house in Benson. Next we were onto Kansas City, then back to a duplex in Omaha, and from there to a place on Brown Street. Beth and I added two human puppies interspersed through the moves: first our daughter Katie, and then our son Rob. Bandit and Buddy accepted their new litter mates without question; and Katie and Rob grew up believing Bandit and Buddy were simply their smaller, furrier siblings who somehow talked through my mouth.

We moved so many times, the dogs began anticipating change as soon as the first cardboard boxes were brought down from the attic. With each box packed, Bandit and Buddy would sigh dramatically, "Here we go again. These humans can't commit to a den." Each time a moving truck parked in front of the house, the dogs stubbornly stationed themselves next to the truck, refusing to come back in the house. "Don't forget about us," they'd say. "We'll just wait right out here as a reminder to take us with you."

Our final move, with kids and dogs in tow, took us to a farm on the outskirts of Omaha. With endless space to run and dig, it was paradise for our litter of puppies.

But time passed and we couldn't do anything to stop it. One day as Katie walked through the living room, I said in my squeaky Bandit voice, "Katie, give me a treat." For the first time she looked at me instead of the dog. "That's you talking," she said.

"I'm the interpreter," I explained. "I speak his language."

She rolled her eyes, but Bandit ended up with a treat.

"Thank you, Daddy, for giving Katie my message," Bandit told me.

I scratched him behind his ears. "Not everyone can speak Dog."

A lifetime can be measured by dogs. As I look back and remember different parts of my life, my memories are forever leashed with which dogs were by my side. The Bandit and Buddy years were some of my favorites. They lived long, full lives, at least from a dog's perspective. From a human perspective, 15 years is the briefest blink, and the older you get, the faster those precious years slip away.

Buddy died first. Bandit, for all his mischief, was lost without his brother. He'd search the house, the yard, whimpering at the spaces Buddy once occupied. Bandit hung on for a little while longer, as if he didn't want to leave us alone. But eventually, even his vibrant spirit faded. The day he passed was the end of an era. Something precious, something irreplaceable had gone with him. The house felt too quiet. Too big. Too empty. Like it waited for paws that would never return. There are moments you look back on in life and wish you could relive. I'd sure give a lot to be able to see Bandit's wagging tail once more, or to see Buddy's expression of patient annoyance.

The loss of our first dogs didn't prevent us from finding more animals to love. Our next dog, Lucy, known as the Highway Husky in local news, didn't come to us easily. Bringing her home was a battle of patience and persistence. The dog seemed to be living between the interstates. It was anyone's guess how she managed to survive. She slipped past animal control time and again, a ghost on the asphalt. Beth pulled over daily to leave food, hoping to earn its trust, but Lucy never let her near. After several weeks of being featured in local news reports, the Humane Society finally darted her. Now famous, the public had a lot of interest in adopting her. Beth had more. Every day Beth showed up at the Humane Society as soon as the doors opened to feed and walk the dog. When they released the Highway Husky for adoption a few weeks later, Beth stood first in line.

We'd been warned to keep Lucy inside, or she'd bolt like a fugitive. But keeping the wind under lock and key would've been easier. She turned the house into a demolition zone, which forced us to exile her to the garage. Walks in the pasture weren't much better. She yanked at the leash, dragging us along for the ride. Finally, we had enough. Either she'd learn to call the farm home, or she'd embark on whatever grand adventure she had in mind. At the far end of the pasture, I took a deep breath, reached down, and unhooked the collar.

We unleashed a storm.

Lucy, quick as lighting, bolted away. We watched, dismayed, as the failed experiment nearly disappeared from view.

Then suddenly, when she reached the end of our property, she made a sharp turn and came right back and sat next to us. She made it known she wasn't a dog any person could control, but she'd decided her home was with us, and she always came back. During her years with us, she vigilantly guarded our house from every bird, squirrel, or deer.

Our Highway Husky numbered among a motley crew of strays and adopted dogs that found a home with us. Around the time Rob started sixth grade, we found ourselves dogless for the first time since we'd brought Bandit home from the pet store. Beth and I both wondered if we should take a break from dogs. Rob wasn't keen on this idea. For his birthday, he wanted just one thing—a dog.

Rob is the type of person who goes to the Humane Society and looks for the least adoptable dog—the mangy one, the hurt one, the one no one else wants. We strolled up to the chicken wire fence surrounding the kennel. One dog in particular stood out. He was white with spots, likely a rat terrier mix. When he saw us, he actually started scaling the fence, finding footholds in the wire until he met us at face level. He demanded our attention.

In the get-acquainted room, we learned the dog could fly. From the top of the couch to the chairs, from the floor to our laps, from one sofa armrest to the next, the dog soared through the air, a bundle of unlimited energy. With leaps and bounds he zoomed, tongue out, to offer flying licks to our faces..

The worker gave a weary smile, as if she'd seen this situation before. "Most dogs get older and lose their energy, but this dog won't. He's already been brought back three times. Unfortunately we don't think he can be trained. He's next on the kill list."

Rob didn't have to hear anything else. He'd found his dog. It took a couple of days before we could bring him home. The adoption required piles of paperwork, a lot of signatures saying we couldn't return the dog no matter what. But finally, that three-time loser, Benny the Wonderdog, found his home.

The smartest dog I'd ever known in my life, Benny had seven or eight distinct barks, and I learned to translate them all. One bark meant "Someone I don't know is in the driveway." Another, "Here comes Daddy." And another, "There's a deer in the pasture," and, "An acorn fell on the roof."

He also mastered English. He knew the names of his toys better than most toddlers. You could say, "Go get Mr. Bubbles," and he'd return, tail wagging, with Mr. Bubbles in his mouth.

Raising Benny didn't stop us from fostering and adopting other dogs along the way. Benny enjoyed their company momentarily, but when he got tired of them, he'd run to the back door and bark "let me out." We'd open the door, and the other dogs would sprint into the backyard. Benny, pausing at the threshold, watched them go, and returned to his place on the couch. "Good God, those dogs are not like us," he'd say.

Benny loved kids. He loved the big birthday parties and commotion when friends came over. At one of these parties, I heard a kid exclaim, "Look how fast this dog can eat a hot dog!"

If food sat on the counter, you couldn't turn your back. Since Benny the Wonderdog could leap tall buildings in a single bound, no food at any height was safe. If you grabbed a potato chip and weren't watching, he'd fly through the air and grab that chip right out of your hand before it reached your mouth.

Benny's belly grew rounder from his unhealthy junk food addictions, but as the Humane Society worker predicted, he never slowed down. He lived longer than any dog I've ever known. If I had to guess, he's currently wearing down the furniture in heaven, zipping from couch to couch. Or more likely, God finally gave him wings, realizing that a Wonderdog like Benny needed to fly.

There's a special place in hell for people who are mean to dogs. Someone at the Humane Society told me a person turned their dog in because it clashed with their new furniture. Dogs are not accessories. They are so much smarter than we give them credit for. They have so much to teach us about life. Dogs live only 15-percent of the average human lifespan, and yet they seem a lot happier than those of us who live until we are 80. I've never known a dog to regret past choices or carry around old disappointments. They are just as happy to see you return from the mailbox as they are if you've been gone for a week.

If we all lived like dogs, the world would be a better place. They live in the moment. They don't worry about much of anything, because they trust we will take care of them. And they know it's their job to take care of us. It's healthy to own a dog. The weight of an animal in your lap melts away the weight on your shoulders.

I've heard people complain, "It's a doggone world," or "This place has gone to the dogs." But to me, that's an endorsement. I'll take a doggone world any day of the week.

I've never heard of dogs fighting over politics or walking into a building and killing a bunch of people. Dogs don't segregate based on fur color or economic status. I haven't always understood people or been able to interpret them; but dogs, I get. And a life with a dog by your side is a life worth living.

HAUNTED BY
THE FRIENDLY GHOST

"Just pull the magic string—you'll never know what they'll say next!"

The commercial sucked me in like a giant fish, and I was Jonah, helpless to look away. I couldn't believe my eyes. There on our 19-inch black and white RCA television set, my favorite cartoon character, Casper the Friendly Ghost, came to life as a plush toy.

"Now your favorite TV characters are talking dolls," the TV announcer said. Entranced, I studied the toys propped upright against a black background—Matty Mattel, Sister Belle, and best of all, Casper.

"They really talk when you pull this magic string!" A disembodied hand reached out and pulled Sister Belle's chord.

"Will you play with me?"

"Let's draw pictures!"

The voiceover continued. "Each one says eleven different things!"

"Let's play cowboy!"

"I can really talk!"

The high-pitched whines of the dolls were interspersed by the low chuckling from the announcer. "The fun is," he said, "you never know what they're going to say next."

Suddenly Casper appeared. "I'm a friendly ghost. Don't be afraid of me."

Forget Matty Mattel and Sister Belle. Casper stood out as the most coveted toy. He wasn't like his mischievous uncles, or the other triangle-headed ghosts in his haunting. Casper just wanted to be friends with people, not terrify them in their beds at night.

"These dolls are your very own friends to play with and talk to," the voice-over said. "Each doll is so soft and cuddly you'll want to take them to bed with you."

I didn't need to hear more.

"Mom?"

I found her in the bathroom, bent over the bathtub, scrubbing oven grates. The smell of ammonia smacked me across the face, and I felt a little woozy. This cleaning process repeated once a quarter in the Osborn house, and usually the smell permeated so strongly I'd sneak out to pee in the alley to avoid the fumes. But this counted as an emergency.

"Mom?" I said again.

"Do you need the bathroom?"

"No."

"Are you hungry? I'm almost done in here. We'll have supper soon."

"I'm not hungry."

"What's wrong, are you sick?"

"I'm fine."

She looked at me, waiting for some explanation.

"I really want a Casper the Friendly Ghost doll," I said, my voice jittery with excitement. "You pull the string and it says eleven ghostly things."

"Is that so?"

"Yes."

"Well, we'll have to see what Santa brings, won't we?" A smile played around her lips.

I floated out of the bathroom, and not only because of the contact high with the ammonia. Christmas was only a couple months away. I'd have plenty of time to write Santa a letter.

Seeing my dream toy in the pages of the Sears Wish Book felt like a step closer to the best Christmas ever. The print ad read: "Loveable Casper the friendly talking ghost, fifteen inches tall, terry cloth costume. Stuffed body, plastic head. Five dollars and ninety-nine cents."

In the 1960s, a week's worth of groceries cost around twenty-five dollars, but for a single mom with four children, we made do with less. Mom canned most of her own vegetables, and what she couldn't can, she froze. She baked bread from scratch, butchered chickens in exchange for free meat, and sacrificed her own meals to make sure we never went hungry. Mom was skinny, but fueled with at least two pots of coffee a day. She worked tirelessly to give us everything we needed.

Mom always awoke before we opened our eyes and stayed up long after we'd drifted to sleep. I never fully grasped what filled those quiet hours; but each morning the house gleamed, unseen chores had been completed, and her rosary laid freshly draped beside her prayer books, next to an empty mug.

My child's mind wasn't big enough to see the extra burdens Christmas could bring to a mom who'd felt the shame of paying with food stamps at the grocery store. Mom eschewed pity. She worked harder than four parents, chose the more arduous detours if she might bump up against someone feeling sorry for her. And while she didn't have much to work with, my siblings and I didn't know a Christmas without decorations, homemade candy, and special touches.

The magic of Christmas was nearly tangible. Mom dressed all four of us children into our best clothes and escorted us to the midnight mass at our local Catholic church. With the melody of "Joy to the World" still playing on the pipe organ, we rushed home and climbed into our beds, anxious to sleep since Santa didn't visit kids while they were awake.

Of course, we didn't stay asleep long. The excitement of Christmas morning provided a powerful shot of adrenaline to the heart. Long before the winter sun peaked over the wind-packed snow, we leapt from our beds and gathered around the pine-scented Christmas tree, amazed at the carefully wrapped packages which must have come straight from the North Pole. I never stopped to wonder at the smell of a turkey already wafting from the oven, nor did I bother to question when Mom had been able to sleep. She'd crafted each detail with such effortless grace that the effort itself was lost on me.

We took turns opening our gifts, and since the youngest went first, I bore the torture of waiting the longest. I scanned the packages, hoping to spot the box which would hold my beloved Casper doll. I'd already imagined the adventures we'd have together. At Casper's suggestion, we'd play cowboy, draw together, and he'd always reassure me he wasn't there to scare me, because he wanted to be my friend.

It felt like a decade passed before my turn. I found a lumpy package held together with Scotch tape. The tag said, "To Donald, From Santa." The shape seemed wrong. Casper came in a box that looked like a haunted house, and his bright plastic face peered through a window in eager anticipation to make new friends. Gingerly I gave the package a little squeeze and felt something soft and pliable between my small fingers. Maybe Santa had taken Casper out of the box before wrapping it?

"Well, come on Donald, let's see what Santa brought," Mom said, her tired eyes reflecting the twinkling lights from the tree.

I tore open the package. Wrapping paper flew across the living room. My heart pounded with hope. But when I saw the homemade doll, tears welled up unbidden. I stared at the doll in my hands, my heart sinking. A lump formed in my throat. I wanted to be happy. I wanted to smile and say thank you, but disappointment pulled me under.

"Look, Santa brought you a Casper the Friendly Ghost," Mom said.

The doll in my hands was decidedly not a Mattel creation. I was not fooled by the intricate hand-stitching. I was not fooled by the velvety cloth covering. I was not fooled by the button eyes and embroidered smile. This was clearly not the product of a big manufacturing company. No plastic packaging. No string to pull. No friendly ghostly sayings.

"Yuck, what is this?" I said.

"It's Casper," Mom said again.

"No it's not." I tossed the toy aside. What a crushing blow. I'd so looked forward to that Casper doll, and now I wallowed in a deep level of self-pity which only another four-year-old could have fully understood. I don't remember my mom's reaction, though I imagine it must have been more crushing for her. The nights I spent sleeping without a care in the world, she'd stayed up late working, caring enough to try to give the world to me. And I'd thrown it away with disgust.

As an adult, I often think back to that Christmas. Mom poured her heart into that doll. She'd done everything within her power to give me what I'd wanted, and I'd been anything but grateful. In my childish desire for the perfect toy, I'd missed the love stitched into every seam. When the memories and regrets resurface, I think of Mom alone at the kitchen table, stuffing love into a doll I wouldn't appreciate until too late.

Mom died in July 2021. During the Rosary service, I stood and told the story of Casper the Friendly Ghost. "I'm not a materialistic person," I said. "But I'd give just about anything to have that Casper doll back."

But even more, I wish for one more Christmas morning with Mom. All these years later, I'm still haunted by the ghost of Christmas Past.

CONCRETE CREATIVITY

When I was around five or six, I found this old concrete breaker, which was basically a big, heavy bar. If you could lift it up high enough and it landed just right, it would break concrete.

The neighbor across the alley was building a garage, and as a result, he had a lot of concrete blocks just sitting around. I couldn't have asked for a better playground. I had an actual construction tool and zero parental supervision.

When no one was around, I hauled my concrete breaker across the alley. I spent hours heaving it over my head and letting it drop. I loved hearing my own power in that reverberating thud, and the feel of the metal's vibrations against my hands. Each satisfying sliver of concrete that worked loose from the block was proof of my hidden superhero talents. This went on for some time until my neighbor caught me in the act one afternoon.

"Hey, what do you have there?" he asked me.

I held up the bar for inspection.

"That's a pretty fine tool," he said.

I nodded.

"Looks like it's pretty effective in breaking up concrete blocks."

I nodded again.

"Are you one of the Osborn kids?" He pointed towards the direction of my house.

"Yeah."

"I see," he said. "Well, I could really use a tool like that." He pulled his wallet out of his back pocket, and I watched with interest as he extracted a crisp one-dollar bill. "What do you say? Do you have any interest in selling it to me?"

My eyes got big seeing that flash of green. I couldn't believe my good fortune. It would be sad to part with the concrete breaker, but this guy was willing to pay me a hundred cents. "Yes, sir!"

I handed over the tool, and he handed over the dollar. I was rich. I couldn't wait to tell all my friends about how I'd facilitated this trade agreement.

Years later I learned the truth of this encounter when I met Bill McCarter. "Hey, I've heard about you," he said.

"Unfortunately, I hear that a lot."

"You used to live across the alley from my grandpa."

"Oh yeah?"

"He said you'd go over there all the time and break up all his concrete, so he bought your concrete breaker so you'd stop it."

That's when it clicked for me. I hadn't negotiated some

big business deal as a five-year-old, I'd been paid off to stop destroying private property. Grandpa McCarter had out-smarted me, but in a way that left me none the wiser.

Kids today have no shortage of toys, but despite this, seem to have high levels of boredom. Apparently it's not possible for a kid to be in a restaurant without some sort of electronic device in front of them. Waiting in line without a phone? Unthinkable. And the idea of walking home from school to play with friends in the backyard? Long-gone. Modern children need to be enrolled in ninja, ballet, violin, soccer, piano, lacrosse, Mandarin, computer coding, and swim team.

I feel sorry for parents these days. There are so many pressures to spend every moment talking and interacting with offspring, ensuring they hear the appropriate daily number of SAT words before they are dropped off at Span-ish immersion preschool. In addition to providing organic, sugar-free foods, parents are supposed to negotiate tan-trums by talking about feelings.

By the time they make it out to a restaurant on a Satur-day night, it's no wonder why parents just hand over the iPad. They are exhausted.

Of course, there were no iPads in the 1960s and 1970s, but you'd better believe my own Mom never hauled enter-tainment to a restaurant. In fact, she never took any of us kids out to eat. Why pay money for something she was per-fectly capable of cooking herself? And there was no money to spend on lessons and after-school activities. There was no expectation Mom would stop working the second we walked in the door to play with us and help us think up creative solutions to any problems we might be having.

Saying "I'm bored" in front of Mom was akin to asking for a broom to sweep the floor or for a bag of potatoes to peel. We didn't have a lot of toys, but we had no shortage of imagination. I remember a lot of details about my childhood, but I don't remember feeling bored.

Today kids have Lego, drones, video games, Power Wheels, Barbie dolls, plastic battery-powered tool sets that make the noises for you. There's no need to imagine the flashing lights and sirens on your toy firetruck, because if you just push this button, it'll do all the work for you. Modern toys leave little to the imagination and negate the need for fantasy.

Though I didn't have a lot of store-bought toys, I made do with what I could find. The concrete breaker wasn't the only found treasure that kept me entertained. I seemed to have a knack for discovering forgotten items and giving them a second life as toys. My first guitar was rescued from a garbage can in that same alley. It had only three strings and a dead mouse inside. Mom wasn't a fan. Every time she caught me with it in the house she'd say, "Get that thing out of here!"

"But I took the mouse out," I explained.

Her look told me not to argue.

I once built a go kart out of all the old wheels I found. And then I turned that go kart into an airplane. I fashioned a wooden board across the front of it and called it a wing. I tried to fly it off the roof. My ribs hurt for weeks. It's amazing what a person can learn about aerodynamics from an experience like that, at least if they live to tell about it. Modern kids don't seem to have as many opportunities to learn by trial and error. Parents are often too quick to intercede. Though I can admit it's probably a step in the right direction in modern parenting to prevent children from driving homemade airplanes off the roof. But I sure learned my lesson in a hurry. After two or three more failed attempts, I learned my go kart not only lacked lift and thrust, but also lacked a hope and a prayer.

I built a fort in the next-door neighbor's shed. Somehow he never found out. Or maybe he just didn't want to pay me off to stop trespassing. Either way, that shed was the headquarters for many adventures.

An old steering wheel became a death-defying swing. I hung it from a tree branch higher than our roof. We could swing from one side of the house to the other. Modern playgrounds would never allow such a magnificent apparatus. Lawyers have ruined playgrounds.

Venturing out of the neighborhood, I found countless materials. I created parachutes, built bigger and better jumps to see how high our Buzz Bikes could fly, and drug casket boxes home from the undertaker and turned them into submarines with periscopes with hand-drawn instrumentation on the inside of the box. Modern kids probably have no idea how much fun can be had with the stuff you find outside a funeral home.

We were cowboys who spent the day on hunting expeditions or chasing down cows on our bicycle horses, only returning home to camp in the backyard with homemade tents.

Anything with a sharp point could become a javelin or an arrow, which would be thrown at targets, or stuck in a neighbor's fence. We made sling shots and played David and Goliath. I could sling a rock half a block with the accuracy of a young Israelite sheep tender. Of course, BB guns were an endless source of entertainment. I don't remember my mom ever reminding me to be careful, and I never did shoot my eye out.

Looking back, there was no end of fun to be had in my childhood. But it wasn't the concrete breaker or any other object that kept me busy. It was the freedom to explore, to imagine. Kids today have less room for their minds to wander and invent. And there's less opportunity for them to jump off the garage roof, unsupervised, holding only a blanket over their heads.

No wonder they are so bored.

THE DING DONG ALTAR BOY

The day Sister Borromeo came into our sixth-grade classroom and tapped me on the shoulder, I felt an instinctive surge of panic. My eyes briefly flicked to my desk, wondering if it might somehow provide refuge from whatever fate awaited me. No doubt she'd found out about one of my latest misdeeds—arson, money-laundering, vandalism, mouthing the words during music class.

She slid into her desk and waited impatiently while I trudged into her office, willing the floor to open up and pull me right through. "Have a seat."

I tenderly lowered myself into the execution chair, looking around for the switch which would send me straight to hell.

"Congratulations, Donald."

Wait. Was I dead already?

"You've been chosen to serve the Lord as an altar boy."

I looked around, sure she'd confused me for the coat

rack in the back corner of the room. "Me?"

"The new altar boy class will be starting soon, and you'll need your mom to sign this permission form."

I gingerly took the paper from her hand, sure it must be an indictment in disguise. I looked it over, and to my surprise, the jumbled mess of words before me did seem to be an invitation to become one of Saint Patrick's newest altar boys.

I flew home from school. "Mom, you aren't going to believe it!"

"There's no need to shout. I'm standing right here."

"Sister Borremeo called me into her office—"

"What now?"

"That's just it—"

"Donald, did you track mud into the house?" She looked down to appraise my shoes, and sure enough dirt clumps left a telltale trail from the screen door to where I stood.

"Go take your shoes off. I'm getting the mop."

"Mom! I'm gonna be an altar boy!"

She stopped in her tracks, turning slowly back to face me. "Telling fibs will not get you out of trouble for dragging dirt into the house."

"It's not a fib. Look." I shoved the paper into her hands.

I studied her eyes as she scanned the paper. Up to that point in my life I don't think I'd ever seen my mother cry— except for the time we found a snake in the garden and set it on the front porch for her to find--but I'd be danged if tears weren't forming right in her dark brown eyes.

I shifted awkwardly, not used to making my mom cry for good reasons.

"Well, this is something," she said. She coughed and rubbed her eyes. "Donald, the priest is about as close to God as you can get. And you'll be standing up there on the altar, right next to the priest."

In the following days, I don't think it was my imagination, but Mom's eyes took on an extra glisten when she looked at me, like maybe all her prayers on my behalf hadn't been for naught. She hardly yelled at me at all when I got into a huge fight with my sister, and for once, she even took my side. Things were looking up.

If I'd thought life couldn't get any better, I about floated to heaven when I found out that in order to complete altar boy training, I'd be released early from school Friday afternoons. This was an extra kick. Anything was better than school.

Sister Borromeo played the part of the priest in training sessions. She led us would-be altar boys through the entire mass. As she lifted her hands over the altar table and chanted the prayers of sacramental blessings, I wondered if she cursed womanhood. Thanks to Eve, a snake, and a double-x chromosome, Sister Borromeo was relegated to a subservient role behind every priest in the diocese. Though she lacked ultimate authority over the church, she held sway over the newest batch of altar boy trainees.

We followed her lead, learning how to assist the priest in setting the altar, carrying the cross, and all the other odds and ends the Pope deemed necessary. Lots to take in, not too much fun, but probably a little more enjoyable than long division. The most dreaded duty for an altar boy was the ringing of the bells at specific moments during the Eucharist prayer. The old church on King Street had three electric buttons resembling piano keys built right into the floor where the altar boy knelt while the priest blessed the Styrofoam crackers and wine. I couldn't quite understand how all the theology worked, but somehow, in the midst of the priest praying and the altar boy pushing those keys to ring the bells, the cracker and wine turned into Christ's body and blood.

A daunting task for a first-time altar boy.

Weeks of practice led to my first real Mass, where there were no do-overs. I showed up to the church, my hair slicked down, ready to take on this task which would hopefully knock off at least a few years of purgatory from my sentence. First time altar boys were always paired with a more experienced boy, called a trainer, and I'd been paired with Kenny Groves. A whole grade older than me, Kenny had been serving as an altar boy for a year. He knew the ropes.

The long, white vestments were kept in a closet. They basically looked like bed sheets with holes in them so you could stick out your head and arms. In training we wore our normal clothes, but today was the real deal—kind of like a dress rehearsal and first performance all in one.

"Here, this one's perfect for you," Kenny said, barely hiding a grin as he passed me the longest robe in the closet.

I didn't argue. The thing draped all the way down to the

ground. "It seems a little long," I said.

"It's fine."

"Yours only comes to your calves," I said.

"It doesn't matter. We've got work to do."

I forgot about my draping robes and we set about our next task, to get the items ready for communion. The wine had to come out of the cupboard and be poured into the sacred chalice, where it would later be turned into blood. Kenny took care of the wine, and by take care of it, I mean he took a big ol' swig of the stuff, straight from the bottle.

"Here," he said, placing the bottle in my hands.

I didn't remember this lesson from Sister Borremeo, but there I stood in the sacristy, performing my first duty as altar boy, taking a gulp of altar wine. It tasted horrible.

We started laughing. "Do you think we are drunk?" I asked Kenny.

In walked Father Deaver. "Which one of you is going to carry the incense burner?"

"Him," Kenny said, pointing at me.

One boy carried the incense burner, and the other transported the wine to the altar. The wine clipped into a tray, which could easily be carried with one hand, whereas the incense burner required some level of concentration. I clutched the delicate container, suspended on its long golden chain. We'd practiced this with Sister Borromeo. Reverently carrying an incense burner required both hands. Part of the chain would extend past your left hand, and in your right hand you'd swing the smoking receptacle.

We lined up at the door, and the music stopped,

signaling our entrance.

Since I carried the incense, I had to walk down the aisle first. I could feel the heat rising up the chain, scorching my right hand. I grimaced, shifting my grip. Kenny pushed me forward. "Go, go," he whispered.

My moment arrived. My first time performing in front of an audience. I stepped forward, but my shoe caught on my robes. "Go," Kenny whisper-yelled.

Both hands occupied by a holy smoking cylinder, my foot caught in my robe, and I had no choice but to move forward. I proceeded towards the altar, kicking my leg out to release my foot from captivity, while swinging the burning incense, creating an awkward, halting gate, tripping, bumbling, and all the while Kenny breathed down the back of my neck, pushing to hurry me along.

Somehow I made it to the altar, only slightly scathed by burns and embarrassment. We sat in the high-backed chairs on either side of Father Deaver, and suddenly it hit me. *Oh shit, I gotta ring that bell.*

Before we'd started our procession down the aisle, Kenny made me a promise. "Don't worry, I'll nod at you when you need to ring the bell." With those words, I'd gazed at Kenny as though he were my personal savior.

"Oh good. I won't have to know when to ring it."

"That's right," Kenny had said. "Just watch for my nod."

Now we knelt behind the priest, with Mass at full throttle. I was pleased as anything to be kneeling up on the altar, close to God, and close to my friend, Kenny.

Speaking of Kenny, what the heck was he doing? A strange rustling sound came from him. I glanced over and spied him fiddling with something inside his robes. Was he trying to signal me? Could this be my moment to ring the bells? It didn't seem right. Wasn't it too early? My breath hitched. This was it—the moment of recognition, the nod that would change everything. While the rest of the congregation bowed their heads in prayer, I'll be damned if Kenny didn't pull out a Hershey's chocolate bar.

Now, this was a grave sin. Catholic doctrine required fasting before taking communion. Sunday mornings, Mom would get us up extra early so we could eat breakfast and still have enough hours pass before the Host could touch our tongues. And now, before my very eyes, my great savior who was going to nod at me to ring the bells, my trainer who taught me to serve the priest and thereby serve God, was sneaking bites of a Hershey's bar.

I was dumbfounded.

The Apostle's Creed was in full force, and I struggled to keep up. With each word, anxiety mounted within me. The time for the bells drew ominously near. For once in my church-going life I willed time to slow down, but in open defiance, the clock moved faster and faster, causing everything around me to pass in a blur.

Father Deaver stood up there doing the Mass things, and I took my place beside the altar to kneel. Pretty soon, Kenny caught my attention and gave his head a quick nod. I reached for the keys. DING! DONG! DING!

The priest stopped. A few awkward titters sounded

from the congregation. Kenny mouthed to me, *Oops.* I'd have liked to disappear inside my too-long white robe.

Mass continued. Kenny nodded again. DING! DONG! DONG! Once more, the most sacred part of the service screeched to an embarrassing halt. Out of the corner of my eye, I could see Kenny's body convulse with laughter. Heroically, he held back the noise which otherwise consumed his adolescent frame.

My first time serving in a Catholic Church, with the weight of at least a hundred people staring at me, not to mention the crucified Jesus Christ watching over the altar, and things were not going well. Kenny and I were probably drunk from our sip of unconsecrated communion wine. I'd almost tripped and burned down the whole church with the incense burner. And now I'd flubbed the bell ringing. Twice.

Kenny emphatically nodded at me again. *Nope,* I said to myself. *I'm not falling for that again.*

Father Deaver stopped the mass for a third time and looked down on me. "Don," he said. "Now is the time to ring the bells."

DONG! DONG! DING!

HANG IT ALL

Hang gliding and Nebraska go together like snowmobiles and Miami. But at eighteen years-old, with sky for brains, I wasn't one to let geography get in the way of a bad idea. I'd been accused of having my head in the clouds, which is where I liked it. I spent my free hours at the airport west of Chadron. Already I'd earned my private and commercial licenses and soon would add my instrument's license to my resume.

Why stay grounded when you can share altitude with the birds? For me, too much time in the sky didn't exist.

So when I heard someone in town had a hang glider for sale, I hopped on my bike and went to investigate. The Mylar canopy stretched out like a Nebraska sunset, all yellows and oranges. I didn't know anything about hang gliders at the time, but figured I could replace any broken or missing pieces with a few trips to the hardware store. The price met my budget, meaning cheap. The cash flew out of my hands.

I suckered my friend Ted Grant into helping me. Built for the sky, the glider proved unwieldy on land, and hauling the thing around required two people. We needed room to assemble the glider and accommodate the fourteen-foot wingspan. The high school football field fit the bill.

While our local hardware store kept a good stock, it didn't have much in the way of hang glider parts. Being resourceful teenage boys, Ted and I scrounged supplies and finagled them to fit our purposes. About half a roll of Duct tape later, we had ourselves what looked like a functional flying machine.

We started looking for a launching spot.

Nebraska isn't known for mountains, but the area around Chadron stands out from the eastern half of the state. For one thing, it defies the cornfield stereotype. Tucked away in the northwestern panhandle, this little piece of heaven is home to rugged cattle lands, wheat fields, badlands, pine-covered ridges, and hiking trails that'll leave you breathless from the exertion as well as the beauty.

While we had more hang-gliding launches than a person might assume at first glance, Ted and I needed practicality. We didn't own a vehicle capable of transporting a fourteen-foot hang glider; more importantly, we didn't want to disassemble it. Like in real estate, we wanted three amenities: location, location, location.

Chadron rests in a well-laid-out grid, nestled between hills, rolling farmlands, and the empty throne of a king. Before the devastating July 2006 fires devoured land and homes and forced half the town to evacuate, King's Chair had been a site to behold. Guarded by majestic Ponderosa pines which had stood sentry since the 1920s, the rock chair bore an uncanny resemblance to a throne.

We started our ascension, lugging the aluminum frame which felt like lead by the time we got to the top. Ted agreed I should be the first one to try the glider, since I'd had the most experience being airborne. Of course, I'd never tried hang gliding in my life. But I knew how to fly a plane. How hard could this be? I stepped into the harness, tightened the straps, double-checked the buckles. I fisted the control bar, gazed out at the town, and formed my mental flight plan. I'd soar over the high school football field, which was a half-mile due north. Then I'd head past the railroad tracks, out towards the Dawes County Fairgrounds, which was another mile and a half, then land out near Frank Snook's airfield where I'd first flown a plane.

"Ready?" Ted asked.

"Absolutely."

I took off running, gaining the momentum I'd need to fly off the hillside and off to my adventures. The wind caught. I felt the lift pull me from the ground.

And then I soared right into a nosedive onto the rutted trail below me.

"Are you okay?" Ted called. He didn't have to shout loud, since I'd practically landed back on top of him.

"I think I'm too heavy," I said. "We need someone lighter."

I had just the person in mind.

We found my little brother Stephen digging for

earthworms in the front yard. Sometimes he'd sell the worms to local fishermen, though he preferred to use them himself. He made even bigger pocket change night-crawler hunting, heading out at dark after it rained, with a pail in one hand and a flashlight in the other. He'd come back with a bucketful of worms and a big smile on his face. Stephen, the youngest Osborn, had a lifetime of practice doing dumb things at the request of older siblings.

"Hey Stevie," I called out. "Wanna try something really cool?"

He tossed the worms in the Styrofoam cooler faster than a fish can swallow a hook.

Soon we were back, picking our way through the tall, itchy grasses on the King's Chair path. "A real hang glider?" Stephen asked. "Does it work?"

"Of course," I said. "I'm just too heavy." At age 18, I probably weighed around 150 pounds soaking wet. Stephen, only 14, hadn't hit his growth spurt yet, though his arms were already wiry with muscle. I'd learned the hard way I could no longer beat him in a wrestling match.

"Whoa, is this it?" Stephen took in the assembled glider, and I had to admit, it looked glorious, the bright colors a delightful contrast against the dark green trees.

"Yep," I said.

"You sure about this?" Ted asked him.

Stephen gave a casual shrug, but he couldn't hide his sense of adventure.

"Let's get you strapped in," I said.

Stephen stepped into the harness, and I showed him

how to pull the straps tight, securing his buckles, making it up as I went along. "I don't want you falling out onto the High Rise Building," I told him. Reaching twelve stories, the college residence hall was the tallest building in town.

"How do you steer this thing?" Stephen asked.

Good question. I hadn't worried about steering during the ten-second nose-plummet I'd experienced, but out of the three of us, it seemed I should be the one to have aeronautics knowledge. "Just kind of swing your body from side to side," I said with more confidence than I felt.

"How do I get back down again?" Stephen asked.

"Just pull the control bar towards you. Are you ready?"

"Sure." He got into position, hanging onto the control bar, while Ted and I got on either side of him, each grasping a wing. I figured my flight failed partially due to a lack of momentum. Three of us running together should do the trick.

"On my count," I said. "One, two, three—"

Off on a dead sprint, we avoided rocks and tree branches. At the steepest spot, Ted and I abruptly stopped. Stephen, however, kept going. Up and up he went, not leaving the troposphere by any stretch of the imagination, but soaring at least four or five feet off the ground, high enough to count as actual flying.

"We did it!" I shouted. Ted and I exchanged high fives, my eyes still glued to the beautiful banner of success making its way to town.

And then, halfway down the hill, the glider changed course.

Like an eagle diving for a fish, the glider went headfirst into the dirt. Then it rolled. Stephen, good and strapped in, tumbled like Evel Knievel, or maybe like Stevie Knievie. The glider lost pieces as it careened farther and faster. When it finally came to a stop, Stephen hung suspended in the harness, looking up at the sky, which had so recently betrayed him.

"Oh my God, are you dead?"

We ran towards him, momentum pushing our legs into a full gallop, worried we'd start to tumble next from the gravity and slope of the hill.

"I don't think so?" came Stephen's voice.

We unhitched the harness, pulled him out, and waited for the birds to stop spinning in circles around his head. With our combined medical expertise, we determined he'd live. Being a tough guy, Stephen wasn't the type to admit pain. "I can walk," he said, wincing.

"Should we try it again?" I asked.

"I dunno." Ted sounded doubtful. "It's pretty busted up. It's gonna take a lot of trips to the hardware store."

"Yeah. Let's gather the pieces. We can work on it tomorrow," I said.

The three of us tracked down as many pieces of the glider as we could find, like an expensive Easter egg hunt. "Hey, I found a screw!" one of us would yell. Once we gathered the pieces, we rolled up the glider and carried it down the hill to Ted's car.

We didn't work on the glider the next day, or ever again. Come to think of it, I'm not sure what happened to it. Likely it sat in the garage taking up space until my Mom got tired of looking at it and sold it at the next rummage sale.

Some dreams soar, some crash, and some end up with a fifty-cent price tag at the rummage sale.

NO MONEY, NO LICENSE, NO PROBLEM

My cousin, John Lliteras, owned a '57 Chevy, and his younger brother, Don, owned a '55 Chevy. Naturally, I set my sights on a '56 Chevy.

Being fourteen and broke never dampened my dreams. John, seeing my determination and a little bit of my desperation, found a 1956 Chevrolet Bel Air in Lusk, Wyoming for fifty dollars. By the time he factored in his retrieval fee, my total came to two-hundred fifty dollars for a car I couldn't even drive.

Besides not being old enough, a few other complications prevented me from sneaking it out onto the highway. For instance, the car didn't have a transmission. Half the engine sat in pieces in the backseat, or at least where the seats should have been, had there been any. The car didn't have half its parts, and the ones it had barely held together. It didn't matter. I owned a car!

As John dragged the dilapidated bucket of bolts into our driveway, I only saw potential in the four-wheel rust sculpture.

I planned to have it up and running by the time I turned 16. Money loomed as an obstacle too steep for me to climb, so I mostly relied on my own wits and any spare parts I scrounged from the junkyard.

John taught me how to rebuild an engine and fix brakes. Hot, summer days had me dripping sweat over my new transmission. In the winter, I learned to rewire the electrical system with half-frozen fingers.

For the first test drive, a couple of my buddies hopped in, and we eased the Chevy onto Third Street. We hadn't gotten around to installing seats, so we sat on turned-over buckets. I gripped the wheel with a thrill buzzing in my veins, punched the gas, then—WHAM! The car catapulted us straight into the backseat, buckets and all.

Later I confiscated bucket seats from a wrecked Chevy Chevelle. I'm not sure where the name 'bucket seats' comes from, since personal experience tells me buckets are actually not great for sitting. However, the Chevelle's seats fit perfectly into the Bel Air, and they never tipped over.

The car served me well. When it ran, it took me everywhere I needed to go. When it didn't, I ran on foot to the junkyard or to John's house for extra parts.

I drove that car from the day I turned sixteen until about three years later when a tree jumped out in front of me one night. Likely intoxication played a role. But the Bel Air's unapologetically hefty steel frame saved me from my own idiocy, and less durable biological construction. After the tree incident, the car never quite ran the same, but it taught me a good lesson: always carry a screwdriver, a can of gas, and a match. The screwdriver is for removing the license plates. The gas and the match? Well… let's just say I've never needed to use them. But it's nice to have options.

I ended up trading the Bel Air for an old pickup truck. Parting with it felt like saying goodbye to a friend. For a kid with empty pockets and big dreams, that Bel Air represented everything I wouldn't give up on. Even now, I half-expect to see it rolling back into my life—like a loyal dog, or a haunted relic.

DEMOLITION MAN

Most people try to avoid car crashes. Some crash purposefully for the entertainment of others.

Guess which category I fall into?

I bought a Dodge Dart from Jim Parr for thirty-five dollars my freshman year in college. It became known as the Parr Car. With very little maintenance, I bet I added 20,000 miles to the odometer. My friends and I liked to take it to the stock car track to test how far to the right we could push the speedometer.

When we saw we could push it pretty far, we then wondered if the Parr Car could fly. We drove it straight off a banked corner. The answer? It could. That little Dart went airborne, landing to the cheers of my friends. Unfortunately, the steering wheel snapped off. No steering wheel? No problem. I installed vice grips on the steering column. Sure, they sometimes snapped off mid-drive, turning into dangerous projectiles, and I learned quickly to keep my fingers clear when the wheel jerked back. But aside from that, it served as a flawless solution.

When it became evident the Parr Car was on its last tire treads, it seemed only natural to give the vehicle one last hurrah. My little brother, Stephen, who shared my love for smashing vehicles, agreed the Parr Car deserved a grand finale. If it could survive our stunts, maybe it could survive a demolition derby, where drivers crash old cars into each other until only one is left running.

We paid the entry fee. We already knew it could take a hit; we wanted to know if it could win.

We just needed to make a few minor adjustments.

First, we replaced the vice grip steering wheel. I figured there'd be enough danger coming at me from outside of the car that I didn't need to also dodge internal threats. Next, we removed the oil filter and plugged it up so it wouldn't tear off and leak during the competition. We cut the rear shock absorbers to force the car to bend up instead of down during collisions. Bending down would mean dragging in the dirt and making it nearly impossible to reverse. If I couldn't back up, I'd be a sitting duck, an easy target for a hard hit.

The rules stated the driver's side door must be painted red. Anyone hitting the driver's side door would be immediately disqualified. The Parr Car was already red. We figured this was an advantage because it would make it harder for the other drivers to know where to aim, giving them a higher chance to get kicked out of the competition. I didn't consider it would also make it easier for me to be smashed along with the vehicle, but like most teenage boys, I was invincible.

The night of the derby, sparks danced under my skin. Through the open window, I inhaled the sound of cheers as I maneuvered the Parr Car into the arena, the gate swinging closed behind us. Spectators packed the grandstand. The last rays of sun gave out and the electric lights buzzed overhead. I eyed the other vehicles, sizing up my competition. I revved the engine. My body hummed with the rumble of vibrations.

The flag dropped and we were off.

Each crash was a symphony of chaos, with the kind of thrill no roller coaster could ever replicate. The crowd shouted their approval. This was a new kind of exhilaration. There I was, destroying property and hearing accolades instead of police sirens.

I plowed into the back of a Chrysler.

A station wagon swerved into my back bumper.

Nothing compared to the shockwaves rushing through me, as if the car's impacts were hardwired to my nerves.

The Parr Car and I kept smashing and bashing, hardly aware of the cars around us transforming into junk heaps. We sustained hit after hit, until it got to the point the car didn't have anywhere left to dent. Still, it kept running.

I was having so much fun, it took me a moment to realize my car was the only one still functioning. They were announcing my name over the loudspeaker.

I parked the car in the center of the arena, ready to step out and take my bow. That's when I noticed. I couldn't move. The car was bent up around me, welding me into place. Arena officials waved over the emergency vehicles. Someone said "jaws of life." I was too high on adrenaline to internalize the panic. I winced at the sound of metal scraping against metal as the Parr Car peeled back around me like a can opener. The cool night air hit my skin. Once the last bit of metal gave way, I climbed out, breathed in my freedom, and the audience roared. I drank in the applause, only sparing a moment of pain at the car's demise.

I walked away $800 richer, which seemed like a good pay off for my original $35 investment. The term 'financial genius' ran through my head.

A few years ago, I did a Google search for the two-door Dodge Dart model I smashed into smithereens. Imagine my surprise when I saw the refurbished models going for upwards of $50,000. It didn't take a calculator to figure out where I might have gone wrong.

Still, no amount of money could buy the experience of crashing a car more than forty-five times to amuse an audience.

CHADRON HIGH CRUISERS

Shortly after Henry Ford rolled out the Model T., cruising down Third Street in Chadron, Nebraska, became a sacred teenage ritual. Kids burned gas from one end of town to the other, using gas stations and liquor stores as turn-around points. The one-and-a-half-mile stretch at thirty miles per hour provided a solid three minutes of excitement—four if you got lucky and caught the one stoplight in town.

I have fond memories of those cruising days.

But the most memorable cruise I ever took in high school wasn't near Third Street.

This was the era of muscle cars—Dodge Chargers, Plymouth Roadrunners, and Chevy Chevelles—all guzzling gas like linebackers at an all-you-can-eat buffet. Their engines growled, their horns announced their presence with authority, and their mere existence made you feel a little cooler just standing near them.

Of course, not everyone could afford a muscle car. I drove a twenty-year-old Chevy Bel Air I got for a couple hundred bucks. With enough duct tape, the thing held together on days when the temperature was perfect, and the wind wasn't blowing. Given the usual conditions in western Nebraska, I walked most places.

Normally it didn't bother me much. My friends were generous with rides, and my buddy, Mike Carson, was perhaps the most generous of all. His dad always bought him the coolest stuff—first a Honda Trail 50 minibike, then the Honda 100. These bikes were shiny and new, and Mike never hesitated to let me ride them around; but God I wanted one. I was so jealous.

Mike's generosity didn't stop at sharing his bikes. His dad's next purchase took things to a whole new level. One day, Mike drove up in front of my house in one of the first Honda Civic models sold in the United States. It had these little 12-inch wheels, a sleek, silver finish, and could get up to 30 miles per gallon. This was an astounding feat next to the muscle cars of the day with their V-8 engines and 8-10 miles per gallon consumption, which calculated to more than twice the trips up and down Third Street.

Mike's little car, with its spunky little 'beep beep' of a horn, sounded more like a Fisher-Price toy compared to the lion roars of the muscle cars. Heads turned when it zipped past Main Street. People commented on its economic properties. During my middle school years, gas prices hovered around $0.35 a gallon, but by the end of high school, we were paying $0.60 a gallon. The Civic looked pretty smart indeed. And if I'd been jealous over Mike's motorcycles, I turned the color of a green bean over that car.

One day, when we should have been in class, Mike and I were sitting in front of Chadron High School, skipping stones on the pavement and talking about girls. My eyes swiveled between the big double doors on the southeast end of the building and to the compact Civic parked nearby. The thought hit me like a bolt of lightning.

I nudged Mike with my elbow, a mischievous grin spreading across my face. "Hey," I said, jerking my head toward the Civic, "you don't think we could..."

Mike's eyes followed mine, and he raised an eyebrow. "I see what you mean," he said, his voice full of excitement and a hint of fear. "Let's give it a try."

Our hearts pounded in unison as we moved quickly but cautiously. The Civic hummed as we maneuvered it onto the sidewalk, its little wheels bumping over the curb. I glanced at Mike, who gripped the steering wheel, his knuckles white. "I think it'll just about work," I said, my voice trembling with adrenaline.

"Okay," Mike replied, eyes wide with anticipation. He sat in the driver's seat, ready to roll, but waiting for my signal. I took a deep breath, feeling the weight of the moment, and then gave him a nod.

With the big double doors propped open, I stood in front of the car, my heart racing. I waved my arm, and Mike adjusted the wheel accordingly. The Civic crept through the school doors. The sound of the engine echoed in the empty hallway. I lifted my arms, indicating Mike should straighten the wheels, glancing nervously over my shoulder to make sure we weren't being watched.

As the Civic's front wheels crossed the threshold, a rush of excitement surged through me. We were in! Unable to contain my grin, I quickly hopped in the passenger side, the car's interior feeling oddly out of place in the school hallway. "Well," I said, turning to Mike with a wide grin, "let's go cruising."

There we were, driving down the hallways of Chadron High School. We eased right and the fluorescent lights reflected off the silver hood as we glided past rows of lockers and what used to be the art room. Then we drove up the long hallway to the right, passing more classrooms. We reached the door of our favorite teacher, Mrs. Simonton, and through the skinny doorway window, spotted her teaching at the blackboard. "Hey, stop the car," I said.

Mike pushed the brakes. I reached over and hit the horn. "Beep, beep!" Mrs. Simonton looked away from the board and casually waved as though it were no big thing. And then she turned into a cartoon character. Her head spiraled around at least three times and her eyes boinged out of her head as though attached by Slinky toys.

"Okay, we'd better move," I said.

We steered right, drove through the commons, took another right, and followed the other hallway, honking and waving. When we reached the double doors, I hopped out and guided Mike through. There was enough clearance on either side we didn't even scratch the rearview mirrors. We parked the car, and sat our butts down back in the commons right before the dismissal bell rang.

All around us, students were talking. "Did you just see that car drive down the hallway?"

We'd become an instant urban legend.

Then we saw Mrs. Simonton. She marched straight towards our table. "I cannot f—ing believe it," she said.

Hearing a teacher cuss was more shocking than the fact we'd gotten away with driving a car through the school.

Years later when Mike had nearly worn out that Honda Civic, I sold my motorcycle and bought it from him. The first thing I did was cruise up and down Third Street. It felt pretty good to be in the driver's seat, but I'll admit, it was only the second-best cruise of my life.

ADRIFT

The Chadron cruise was just about the cheapest entertainment in town. Shove three or four teens in a car, pay $1.50 for a six-pack of beer, split $2 of gas, and the fun lasted all night. We'd meet in a parking lot, drink each other's beers, talk and laugh, and then cruise up and down Third street countless times. This was in the years before M.A.D.D., S.A.D.D., common sense, and gas inflation. Now I can't decide which idea was the dumbest—drinking and driving, or spending all that money on gas to not go anywhere in particular. But in the dawn of the '80s, we were more worried about getting nuked by the Soviets than the consequences of our own bad decisions.

The cruise served as our social pipeline. In a small town with little else to do, everyone kept tabs on everyone. People took notice if a car held only two people instead of four, or if it parked suspiciously far from the group. Rumors and romance swirled like exhaust.

Winter made things trickier. Nobody wanted to face the freezing temperatures past sundown. So we'd park our cars in a tight line, roll down the windows just enough to hear through the hum of idling engines, and shout messages from car to car.

"Hey, ask Cindy if she'll meet Petey at the movies Friday night," someone would shout, no concern at all that Cindy was parked three cars down the line.

By the time the message snaked through mufflers and chaos, it arrived at Cindy's ears as: "Percy wants to beat you into a slushy on fight night."

No car was more popular than Bill McCarter's. The guy could chug a case of beer faster than anyone I knew. Consequently, he kept his car well-stocked with a cooler of bargain brews. If you were one of the chosen to ride along with him, it would only cost you about a dollar in gas money, and the drinks were free.

One afternoon, Bill was nowhere to be found, so I'd hopped in a car with other friends. Already I was three or four dollars in for beer and gas. It was only around five o'clock, but dark as midnight and colder than a pretty girl's rejection. Earlier in the week, it snowed enough to keep the plows busy, but not enough to keep Nebraskans from driving—so probably around two feet worth.

Driving by Charlie's Liquor on the west side of town, I spotted Bill's car idling in the parking lot. "Hey," I said. "That's McCarter's car. Pull over."

The plows had scraped the lot free of snow, but left behind a Mount Everest drift right next to the building. We pulled into the lot, skidding slightly as we came up to Bill's car. Bill was nowhere to be seen, but he'd left the car engine running. Back in those days, it was common knowledge Nebraskans only locked their car during the summer months, and this was solely to keep someone from leaving bushels of zucchini in the front seat. Being this was winter, people usually didn't have much to worry about. That night was the exception.

"He's probably in buying beer," I said.

"Should we wait for him?" my friends asked.

"Nah," I said. "I have a better idea."

Hopping out of the car, I motioned to my friends. "Watch this." Had I been holding a beer, I probably would have asked them to hold it.

I jumped in the front seat of the big sedan and put it into gear. Gunning the engine, I aimed straight towards the snow drift. The engine's power gave me just enough momentum to reach the top. It was like a one man's game of king of the hill, and I'd won. The snowdrift was twelve-feet high if it was an inch, and it took a bit of effort to get the door open. Climbing out of the car, I laughed ice crystal tears into the air and half-stumbled down the drift.

A couple of my friends stood watching. They hooted so hard their tears just about froze to their faces. "Oh my God, what's Bill going to do when he sees this?" We nearly had stomach cramps from all the hilarity.

Just then Bill McCarter pulled up, his headlights cutting through the snowy haze.

He rolled his window down, taking in the situation, his

eyes scanning the car teetering on top of the drift. "What's so funny?" he asked. "Whose car is that?"

My stomach dropped. I was seeing double. But if Bill's car was right here then . . .

My friend, who was driving the other car, cursed. It didn't take him more than two seconds to figure out what we'd done. Faster than you could say 'illegal parking spot,' he slammed the gas pedal and shot out of the lot, leaving the rest of us stranded in the frost.

We stared at each other, the laughter frozen in our throats. Slipping on the ice, we grabbed Bill's door handles and flung ourselves into his car. "Go! Go! Go! Go!" we yelled.

Bill didn't question the urgency in our voices. He put the pedal to the metal. We made record time down Third Street, catching Bill up on our escapades by the time we reached the Chuck Wagon east of town. The excitement of the stunt faded, replaced with a kind of nervous energy. That car was stuck. Someone was going to have to deal with it.

"Let's go back and see what's happening," Bill suggested.

He had the keys. We were at his disposal and just as curious, so he drove back the way we'd just come. Now there was activity in the parking lot at Charlie's Liquor. Several people gathered around, surveying the suspended car. We cruised again. Each time we drove by, there was something new to see. "Look, now they have ropes," one of us said. "They're going to try to pull the car off the drift."

The next pass, the scene changed. "Oh man, looks like drift collapsed when they pulled the car off."

"The car is half buried in snow."

"Those poor bastards."

Throughout the evening, we watched their progress, driving up and down Third Street, drinking Bill's beer.

We rolled past one last time. Now the men all had shovels. Snow flew every which way as they tried to free the car from its arctic captivity. The snowdrift looked a bit like the Mammoth Site up in Hot Springs, South Dakota, only instead of fossils, they were excavating a Bill McCarter lookalike car.

"They've been working really hard," we mused. "Think they're thirsty?"

We never did figure out whose car it was. Maybe it was some unlucky tourist, or someone who learned a hard lesson about leaving their car idling in a parking lot. Either way we kept cruising, chasing laughs down Third Street.

If you ever find yourself driving through Chadron, make sure your car doesn't look anything like Bill McCarter's.

SNEAKING INTO STARLITE

Half of Chadron's population must have snuck into the Starlite Drive-In Theater during its years of operation .

The other half was conceived there.

Money wasn't the issue. It only cost a buck or two for entry; though a carload was around $5, and there were no regulations against bending the laws of physics. You could smash as many bodies as you wanted inside each vehicle, as long as you could get the door closed. Sneaking in had nothing to do with monetary constraints, but everything to do with entertainment.

Ingenious methods of sneaking into the drive-in became the stuff of high school lore. We had an unspoken rule of one-upmanship—who could come up with the most incredible solution to watch the movie without opening their wallets.

Mike Carson had an old mail van. We fashioned it with a false back, so when the ticket taker would pull open the back door, he'd see an empty vehicle. But what he wouldn't see was ten kids crammed tighter than a deck of cards, sharing carbon dioxide behind the flimsy wall. Mike would pay for a single ticket, and then once we were parked, the rest of us would pop out and watch the movie.

Kenny Nixon drove a long, black car. Right before he pulled up to the ticket booth, the rest of us would exit on the opposite side. We'd crouch down and strain our knees, walking slowly beside the car, careful to keep our heads below the windows. As the car inched forward, we'd keep pace with the wheels, hidden from sight until we reached our space.

A lot of people hid in trunks, but the box office attendants caught onto that trick quickly. Cars in the 1970s were a lot bigger than they are now, so the floorboards and a blanket made for an easy cover. Plenty of people climbed the fence, but you had to be sneaky about it. They had it set up so cars could only drive in through the entry and out through the exit. Like a rental car company, the exit featured spikes designed to blow your wheels if you tried to drive through the wrong way. Kenny Groves and I once laid a big piece of board over the spikes, and entered in the back way.

But it turned out our most creative form of sneaking in first required us to sneak something out.

During my senior year in high school, my friends found a thick spool of speaker wire—at least three-and-a-half football fields in length—and it gave me an idea. Each drive-in space consisted of a post with a speaker. You'd take the speaker from its holster and slide it into your car, thereby providing you with sound. "You know," I said, "with a long enough speaker wire, you could run it all the way up that hill over there, and you could see and hear all the movies without having to go past the ticket booth at all."

Everyone loved my idea. The next time I entered the drive-in was with a legitimately-purchased ticket and a pair of wire cutters. By the time the second feature came to an end, I'd jerry-rigged the speaker to the new, longer wire, snaked it through the fence, and passed it off to my friends, who walked it up the hill.

It worked beautifully. We tried to keep it a secret, but word got around, and it became the party place. Kids would show up with blankets, beer, and watch movies for free past midnight. Sadly, it didn't last long. Someone must have gotten wise to the idea, because we showed up one night to find the speaker and wire gone. At least we were legends while it lasted.

Though half the fun of the drive-in was sneaking in, the movies weren't half-bad either. It was at the Starlite I first saw John Wayne gallop across a rugged landscape. I tried to keep my cool when Alfred Hitchcock's *Birds* turned the screen black. Ted Grant and I laughed until we couldn't breathe during Don Knotts's portrayal of a hapless astronaut in *The Apple Dumpling Gang*. The most memorable moment happened during *The Texas Chainsaw Massacre* when Kenny Groves ran up and down the aisles with his chainsaw buzzing, all the girls screaming and yelling.

To an onlooker, we looked like a ramshackle car lot in a field on the edge of town, but to the people inside the drive-in, we were transported to other worlds. We'd sit in our cars with the windows open, or on blankets on the ground, inhaling the scent of freshly-cut summer grass mixing with butter and popcorn. The wind carried the dissipating smell of car exhaust and leaded gasoline. The Starlite smelled like youth, like Avon perfumes and nervous energy, like Ponds Cold Cream and Dial soap. Sometimes you'd get a whiff of a dill pickle from the concession stand or the tempting scent of a chocolate candy bar. But the real draw was having the perfect alibi for stretched curfews. Everybody would tell their parents they'd be at the Starlite for the evening, and since the double features usually played until past midnight, we could stay out later. Besides movies, the Starlite provided another outlet of fun for us miscreants. Outside the theater, they kept a massive marquee updated by the staff using ladders and long poles. Each week, as we checked the new movie listings, our brains would buzz with anagrams. We'd cruise up and down Third Street, brainstorming the perfect letter combinations. It would be a good night's project trying to figure out how the letters of each word could be manipulated for our amusement.

When night fell—dark enough to avoid detection but still light enough for visibility—we'd monkey our way to the top of the marquee with no assistance from ladders. We didn't have poles or tools of any kind. It took teamwork, upper body strength, and enough teenage stupidity to make us think we wouldn't get caught. One person would hold the letters, another would pop them into place, and someone else would direct from the ground. We took great delight in rearranging the letters into words which wouldn't be allowed in most Scrabble games. My favorite letter combination of all time had to be 'John Wayne in *The Train Robbers*.' With some creative spelling and a few upside-down letters, the marquee proudly displayed: Johns Rubber Weiny.

The owners must have hated our shenanigans equally as much as we loved them. Sadly, the Starlite Drive-In marquee, once a canvas for our mischievous creativity, eventually only read "Closed for Good." We didn't even bother rearranging the words to spell "Cool doGs freed." It wasn't just a movie theater that closed; it was the end of an era. I'm not sure it ever occurred to us we'd personally accelerated its bankruptcy, but at least we did it with style.

Every now and then when I catch the fragrance of popcorn mixed with fresh Nebraska air or hear the distant hum of a chainsaw, I'm transported back to those nights under the stars. The Starlite may have flickered out, but the memories still shine bright.

OSBORN ON-AIR

No one in Chadron was surprised when I was hired as an on-air personality for the KCSR AM 610 radio station.

Show me a microphone, and I'll reach out my hand. The bigger the audience, the bigger my comfort levels. Speaking on-air to the whole town came almost as naturally as flying on air. Pilots make critical decisions while flying, and radio personalities make on-the-fly decisions.

I worked at the radio station from the time I turned fifteen until I graduated from college. Sitting at those control panels taught me a great deal and provided essential lessons which would later serve me in my flying career.

I learned the value of quick thinking, taking action, and leaving a mark.

Quick Thinking

Sunday mornings on the KCSR airwaves were reserved for religious content. Everything from Gospel music to the Billy Graham Power Hour flowed through stereos across town. One of the more noteworthy broadcasts unique to Chadron in the 1970s, was the Lakota Gospel Broadcast. Only around six thousand people speak Lakota out of the eight billion on the planet. To lose a language is to lose a culture; and the Lakota Gospel Broadcast aimed to keep its culture alive.

At the time, Chadron was the only town within 90 miles of the Pine Ridge Indian Reservation with radio waves strong enough to reach the heart of the Lakota Nation. The Lakota Gospel Broadcast was not only a good money maker for the radio station, but it also played an essential role in resuscitating a dying language.

But getting the recordings for the broadcast was easier said than done.

A Lakota minister, who lived on the reservation, recorded the program each Wednesday. He was a great guy. He always had a kind word for everyone in the station, liked to stop and chat, and was invested in people's lives. No wonder he became a minister. One of the nicest guys around, and also one of the most unreliable. He focused on people, not schedules.

Each Sunday I was responsible for setting up the reels for the religious programming and announcing the introductions live on-air. The standard intro for the Lakota Gospel Show featured traditional drumming and chanting. As the stirring music began to play, I'd voice-over, "Welcome to the Lakota Gospel Broadcast, the only known radio show recorded completely in the Lakota Language."

You could almost hear radios being turned off across

town, because unless you were among the rare few fluent in Lakota, the broadcast sounded like an incompressible river of sounds.

One Sunday I showed up in the studio with the Lakota recording nowhere in sight. The minister hadn't shown up the previous Wednesday. I didn't know what else to do, so I replayed the previous week's episode. This went on for a couple more weeks. Each Sunday I had no choice but to thread the same tape into the machine. No one called in to complain.

Finally, after three missed Wednesdays, the minister appeared back in the studio. "What do you mean you played the same recording three weeks in a row?" he asked, his voice heavy with disbelief.

I swallowed hard, suddenly finding the carpet worthy of inspection. "I didn't have another recording," I mumbled.

"Hmmm," he said, as though to contemplate the situation. "We can't do that anymore."

"No sir," I said.

He paused, perhaps to acknowledge his own contribution to my conundrum. "I'll record two tapes today," he said. "One for this Sunday, and the other as a standby. But, after you play the tapes, I want them erased."

Me being 16, and he being an adult, I agreed to the arrangement.

Three more nerve-wracking Wednesdays passed with the minister as a no-show. By Sunday morning, the station felt like a furnace. As the time to announce the Lakota

Gospel Broadcast ticked down, panic surged through me. I didn't have a reel to play. Sweat oozed from my forehead.

Reel-to-reel players were simple machines: two plastic reels, side-by-side, with a roll of mylar tape winding between them. They could be played forwards or backwards. Most of the tapes we received at the radio show were black or clear in color, but the Billy Graham Power Hour recording always came on a bright red reel.

The final chorus of *Soon and Very Soon* rode the sound waves, indicating the time for me to jump into action. Nausea settled in. I couldn't say 'hello' in Lakota, let alone deliver a 15-minute Gospel presentation in the language. Then again, most of our listeners, not to mention the vast majority of the entire world, couldn't speak Lakota either.

Could I fake a power outage? Pretend to faint? Flee to Canada and start fresh as a maple syrup farmer?

Then my gaze landed on the red reel. Salvation. My heart pounded like a drum circle in full swing as I lunged for it. The music swelled, and I began the intro as usual: "Welcome to the Lakota Gospel Broadcast, the only known radio show recorded completely in the Lakota Language." Then I hit play—and immediately switched the machine to reverse. Listening to Billy Graham preach backwards didn't exactly sound like Lakota—but it didn't sound like English either.

Thirteen minutes passed by, and I leaned back in my chair and listened for subliminal messages within the gobblygook of the country's most famous preacher. It sounded a bit like Billy Graham was being held upside down in the water of the City Dams south of town. I couldn't make out any of the words, but I imagined that if there were hidden messages in the recording, they said something like, *"Don, you are a genius."*

About that time, the station manager, Lee Hall, happened to be walking through the control room. He saw me through the clear glass walls and offered a nonchalant wave. I waved back. Lee stopped, did a double take and locked eyes on the spinning red reel. And then suddenly, as though he himself got switched to reverse, Lee walked backwards, pressed his face to the glass, and bolted into the control room faster than I could push stop.

"Oh my God! That's been running for almost fifteen minutes? How many people have called in?"

"Not a one," I said.

Seeing Lee was about to blow steam out his ears, I flipped on the microphone. As ticked as Lee was, he couldn't yell at me when I was live on-air. "You've been listening to the Lakota Gospel Broadcast," I said. "Join us next week for another edition." I stopped the tape, hit the fast rewind button, and restarted the reel. "Welcome to the Billy Graham Power Hour, a time of inspiration and spiritual renewal. Join us as we explore the teachings of the Bible and hear from Dr. Billy Graham, one of the most respected voices in Christianity."

Once the mic went off, Lee tore into me. "Don't you ever pull something like that again!"

"Yes sir," I said.

He started to storm out, then stopped at the door,

turned, and with a quiet smile said, "If you tell anyone I said this, I'll never admit it, but... what an idea. You're probably going to make it in this world."

Taking Action

Ed Davenport, KCSR Radio engineer, demonstrated a life of action. He kept all the old equipment running and invented contraptions to jerry-rig and improvise machinery in order to squeeze a few more years out of it. Ed alone knew all the secrets to the widgets, gadgets, and electronic paraphernalia that kept AM 610 on the air.

Working as an on-air personality wasn't my only job at the radio. I also served as Ed's assistant when he needed an extra hand. Of course, Ed performed all the duties requiring skilled labor, but even as his grunt man, I watched and tried to learn.

One day, an unsettling silence enveloped the radio station—and not just because I sat in the soundproof control room. Ed was out of town. Lee Hall left for vacation that morning. The rest of the staff already went home for the day. But the silence extended beyond the empty building. The broadcast had stopped. We had dead air.

Every second of dead air bled money. Lost ads, potential FCC fines, pissed-off listeners. But all I could think about? My own ass—squarely on the line.

Instinct told me the station had blown a magnetron tube. As a teenager, I understood one thing: no tube, no radio.

I'd watched Ed change this tube once, and it seemed simple enough. Without a backwards glance, I barged out the door and drove the KCSR Gremlin to the transmitter just west of town.

The radio couldn't transmit without a working magnetron tube. These tubes used magnetic fields to generate high-frequency electromagnetic waves, a technology that later led to the microwave. At the radio station, these tubes were crucial for generating the microwave signals that amplified and transmitted our broadcast over long distances.

When I arrived at the transmitter, it took only a moment to find the problem. Just as I suspected, the magnetron tube was as dead as last week's headlines. *Oh good,* I thought, *I know how to do this.* I carefully untwisted the damaged tube, proud of how easily it dislodged in my hand. *Nothing to this.* I inwardly thanked Ed for his foresight in leaving a box of three new tubes within easy reach. Slowly, carefully, I lifted one of the brand new tubes out of the box, knowing I held about a thousand dollars in my hand. Comparatively, the Gremlin I'd arrived in cost about $2,200 brand new. You'd never find a magnetron tube in the bargain section.

I twisted the tube into place with the delicacy of a surgeon, just as I'd seen Ed do. Almost immediately, the radio turned on and began transmitting.

Don, you are a genius.

POP!

The magnetron tube blew up.

Don, you are an idiot.

Perhaps I twisted it too tightly? I reached for a second tube, even more painstakingly this time, willing my fingers to steady as I secured the tube in place. Again, the radio resurrected to life. I held my breath. The radio continued transmitting. The first tube must have been a dud. Time to hop back in the car and hurry back to the radio station.

POP!

The second tube blew. In the span of five minutes, I'd nearly cost the radio station the price of a brand-new car.

I panicked. Cell phones didn't exist in 1973. When the boss went on vacation, he couldn't be reached. As for Ed, I didn't even know his number. All the staff had flown the coop for the day, and none of them had the technical know-how to handle this situation anyway. Each second that ticked by cost the radio station more money.

I grabbed the third tube.

My hands shook. I handled the tube like a stick of lit dynamite. I snapped it into place, twisting firmly, praying under my breath. Nothing happened. *Oh no, oh no, oh no.* Something looked different. The transmitter had shifted into the down/off position. With one last desperate shove, I pushed it back up. An agonizing second passed.

Click.

A burst of static. Lights flickered.

The dead air rose back to life.

I nearly passed out from relief.

About a week and a half later my boss returned from his vacation. He called me into his office. "Sit down," he ordered.

I took the seat across from his desk, fidgeting in the hard-backed chair.

"I hear you got us back on the air while I was gone."

"Yes, sir. I did."

"Do you have any idea how much those tubes cost?" he asked, his eyes pounding into me.

"Yeah, they're a thousand bucks a piece."

"I'm curious," he said, "what exactly was your thought process? You torched two grand in five minutes. What gave you the balls to think, 'Third time's the charm'?"

I strangled my hands together. "I didn't know what else to do."

He took a deep breath and leaned back, his chair creaking in protest. "Here's what I want to tell you. Throughout my life, the most successful people are the people who get up and do something. Most people would have sat back and done nothing and let us be off the air for days. You should be commended for that. Even though you cost the radio station two-thousand dollars, you didn't just sit there and wring your hands. You faced the situation. I'd much rather see someone try and fail than to not try anything."

I couldn't believe it. I stuttered a thank you, floated off the chair, and headed for the door.

"Do you know why you blew those first two tubes?" he asked, stopping me in my tracks.

"No, sir."

"The transmitter must be powered down before you replace the tube. That second tube you put in there must have blown hard enough it knocked out a circuit and powered down the transmitter. That's why the third tube took, and why you had to power the transmitter back up."

I took in the words. Dumb luck had saved my butt.

Lee's lessons reached far beyond any radio transmission. As an adult, I've tried to follow his words of wisdom. Not every attempt has been successful, but I've learned that action—any action—is always better than doing nothing.

Leaving a Mark

We found endless entertainment in trying to make another radio host laugh during a live broadcast. No one mastered a stoic face like our news director, Mary. Her voice dripped honey, but you didn't want to get stuck on her bad side. She took her job seriously. If the apocalypse arrived mid-broadcast, she'd probably finish the weather report before acknowledging the end times. You could say she was the rock of the station, or more accurately, the boulder. Heavyset, square, and unmovable, Mary wasn't messing around when it came to her broadcast.

Of course, this made the challenge to make her laugh all the more delicious.

Mary stood at the script board, reading a serious news story straight from the *AP Wire,* which presented a good opportunity. Our salesman, Verlan, slid into the room with the stealth of a ninja. Creeping behind Mary, he reached up and tucked her dress into her pantyhose. She didn't blink an eye or pause at a comma. Casually she reached back, plucked her dress out, and went on reading as though the salesman hadn't just exposed her backside.

Verlan needed a Plan B. We pressed our faces against the glass, watching Verlan wiggle something out of his pocket.

"Good gracious, is that a lighter?"

"He's not going to start her on fire, is he?"

Was Verlan a complete sadist? We weren't sure. And yet, not a single one of us moved to stop him. We watched in horror as he flicked the lighter once, twice, and finally a flame jumped to life. His hand reached out, the flame hovering closer and closer to Mary. Had this gone too far? But his hand reached past the hem of her skirt.

"Oh geez," someone said, realizing Verlan's plan.

He held the flame under the ticker tape until the edge of the paper turned black, then orange. The fire crawled higher.

Rattling paper over the radio sounds like a roof caving in. Most people in Mary's situation would have rattled and crumpled the paper to bits. But Mary remained an iceberg. She smothered the flames and put out the fire without even wrinkling the page. She finished her sentence, reached over, and snapped a button on the control board.

Everyone went silent.

Verlan rolled around on the floor, a pressure cooker about to explode. She bent over and looked him in the eye. "Verlan, you are an asshole."

She swiveled back to the control panel, and only then did we see her composure slip. Her face slackened like candle wax. She mouthed what looked like "Oh duck." Mary, still live on-air, had just committed one of the seven deadly sins of radio.

Angrily she shook her head, as though dislodging the past five minutes from her memory, and grabbed the blackened ticker tape. "The weather today is partly sunny . . ."

Verlan got plenty of high fives and momentary fame. But as the ad salesman, it was Verlan's job to read the funeral announcements on-air since he'd been the one to sell the sponsorship to Chamberlain Chapel, the local mortuary. If there was any time you didn't want to break up laughing on live radio, it was while reading an obituary.

Mary sat next door in the production room, but since the walls were glass, she could see Verlan standing over the mic, reading the day's death notices. Finally, she saw her chance for revenge.

She climbed up on the desk, turned her backside towards Verlan, pulled down her pantyhose, and hoisted her dress. She stuck her butt right up against the glass.

Verlan's face turned ketchup-red—good enough to dip a fry in. His lips trembled. His chest heaved. Still, he held back laughter, stiffly reading who survived whom and where to send flowers. Mary pulled her buttocks away from the glass, and though the room was soundproof, Verlan could almost hear the sucking sound as her skin disengaged. His composure cracked but didn't break. As Mary bent over to pull up her pantyhose, Verlan noticed she'd left behind a butt smudge on the glass which could have been a modern art exhibit. Mary not only got revenge. She left her mark. The imprint of Mary's big round ass was more than he could bear.

He squeezed out one final sentence, sounding like someone held his neck in a vice grip. The next funeral announcement would be for himself, the radio announcer who choked on his own laughter.

Verlan swatted at the control board, haphazardly making contact with the mic button. The funeral announcements ended early that day and went straight to commercial. Verlan broke, and he broke hard. His shrieks of laughter penetrated the soundproof glass.

By this time, the whole station was in such a fit of laughter no one could pull it together. For the next twenty minutes, we played records and commercials, because no one possessed enough composure to talk live, not even Mary.

I have fond memories of my years at the radio station, of the people I worked with, and the lessons I learned. Quick thinking and taking action have remained skills throughout my career and life. But in the art of truly leaving a mark, I remain a humble student of Mary's masterclass.

TIMBER!

It wasn't as though we didn't understand the instructions. It was more the procedure we disagreed with.

My best friend, Kenny Groves, and I often did work for his dad, Dick. Built like a bulldog, Dick's bite matched his bark. He was tougher than a railroad spike, and you never saw the man without a cheek full of Red Man Chewing Tobacco.

Dick started his tree business in Chadron as a side gig to his railroad career. At the time, it wasn't uncommon to send a couple of fourteen and fifteen-year-old kids to a worksite with heavy machinery. Kenny and I were hard workers and we already knew about heavy machinery. Some might've even called us good kids—assuming they were well-compensated for their opinion. Truth be told, Kenny secretly taught me to drive the big winch truck up and down the alleys at an even younger age. More than one dumpster succumbed as collateral damage in this educational experience.

(My lawyer assures me the statutes of limitations have passed on underage driving and destruction of public property.)

So there we were, Kenny and I standing in the customer's yard, sizing up the thirty-foot elm tree, and contemplating the procedure. The job was simple enough. They wanted the tree removed. Dick had been clear with his instructions. We were to take the ladder, lean it against the tree, and start removing the branches.

"I think there might be a better way," Kenny mused.

"Your dad said to just remove the branches," I reminded him, not so sure I wanted to cross Dick. Kenny's dad didn't succeed in his line of work with a laid-back personality. "He said he'd finish it off with that new chainsaw."

"But, what if there wasn't a job to finish?" Kenny asked. "What if we finished it before he even got here?"

I glanced between the tree and the rusty saw in my hand. "How do you figure? I'm not sure we can saw that fast."

"What if we didn't saw the branches off at all?"

"Kenny, I know it's hot out here, but I didn't think it was quite hot enough to fry brain cells."

"I'm serious. Look," he pointed at the winch cable hooked to the truck. "I bet if we got that cable high enough into the tree, we could just pull the whole tree over with one big cut at the bottom, save ourselves the trouble of cutting all those branches."

"Now that's a good idea," I said, catching on. We huddled together for a professional safety discussion—meaning we repeated a few warnings we'd heard from adults, nodded seriously, and got to work. If the cable was high enough and tight enough, then when the tree started tipping, we'd pull the truck forward to make sure the tree fell away from the house.

"It'll fall right there," I said, pointing.

Kenny nodded. "It won't even hit the driveway. We'll save ourselves a lot in cleanup."

It took some time, but we secured the cable to the top of the tree.

"You drive," Kenny said.

"You sure?"

"Yep. I'll do the cutting. You keep the cable nice and tight, and when it starts to fall over, you pull forward real fast."

"Got it."

I climbed into the driver's seat of the old 50-series beast which wasn't actually a proper winch truck. What Dick lacked in actual tree-cutting equipment, he made up for in ingenuity. He welded a big A-frame onto the back, running the winch cable over the bottom of the frame. Since he didn't own a woodchipper or any such fancy equipment, the truck also doubled as a way to haul branches to the dump.

The truck's engine rumbled, and I gave Kenny a thumbs up. He signaled back to me and set his saw in motion. Kenny bent low, trying to cut the tree as close to the ground as possible. The hypnotic back and forth of the saw's teeth gnawing into the wood set my mind to wandering. Only a few clouds skimmed the otherwise clear sky. I imagined how the tree would look from above. If I'd been in a plane, I could swoop down over this house and surprise the hell out of Kenny. I grinned, imagining his face. The roar of the airplane engine would overpower any chainsaw. Kenny would look up and—

"Pull! Pull! Pull!"

I startled back to reality. He couldn't have been through the tree already. The old elm tree must have been rotted, because a glance at Kenny told me he was only a third of the way through. The tree didn't know this, however, and shook as though caught in a summer storm.

"Pull!" Kenny shouted again.

Wide-eyed, I saw the tree begin to tip. My foot already rested on the brake with the truck stalled in neutral. I stepped on the clutch to put the truck in gear. Now Kenny yelled with a new intensity. I turned around and instantly saw my mistake. With the truck in neutral the cable slackened, and the tree swayed precariously in the wrong direction.

"Go!" Kenny screamed.

I punched the pedal to the floorboard with all my power. Another mistake. The sudden jolt forward snapped the cable in half. That's when the worst-case scenario played out in front of us. Kenny ran for cover. I gripped the steering wheel as if by sheer force I could turn this whole situation around.

I may as well have gripped at air.

The rotted-out elm still had some fight left in it. It

plummeted into the customer's roof with a ferocious thunder, obviously out for revenge.

And it didn't stop with the roof. The tree hit so hard, the outside wall crumbled, leaving behind a big enough hole we could look inside and see the family looking back out at us.

Like a war scene, dust and debris flew every which way. The people looked shell shocked. They didn't seem to be able to form words, but it wasn't hard to read the looks of horror across their dirt-streaked faces.

Just then, Dick pulled up with his chainsaw. We'd entered a state of shock. We'd been told to take down a couple of branches, but here we'd taken down the whole tree and part of the house as well.

Dick rolled down his window. He took in the tree, the damage, the family staring out at us through the giant hole in their house. He reached into his mouth and pulled out that big black wad of chew. "Well, I'll be go to hell," he said.

He looked to Kenny. "You tell them I'll be back," he said, motioning towards the customers. "I'll talk to them in a bit."

And he drove away.

Kenny and I looked at each other. We looked at the collapsed roof. We looked at the broken tree, with most of the branches still attached. We looked at the customers. They'd inched forward, sticking their heads out the hole to inspect the damage.

"Um," Kenny said, giving them a wave. "My dad said he'll be back soon to talk to you."

Then Kenny ran to the truck, hopped into the passenger seat. "Go!" he said.

"Are you sure I should drive?"

"Let's just get out of here."

I didn't argue. We'd never wanted to leave a place faster.

We drove straight to Kenny's house. We parked the winch truck out front. Had we been smarter, we might have driven that truck straight out of town. We probably should have kept driving until we ran out of gas and then took our chances wherever that landed us.

It seemed a lot safer than what we were about to face.

I hadn't grown up with a father, so I didn't understand the horror in a mother's words: "Just wait until your dad comes home." My mom took care of the beatings herself. But that day I got an inkling of the purgatory associated with waiting for punishment. With each anticipatory minute, I almost longed for the hell fires rather than anything Dick might dole out.

Finally, we heard the rumble of the diesel truck out front. Kenny turned a unique shade of green. I thought I might pee my pants.

The door opened, and for a moment Dick's silhouette blocked out the sun.

He came inside. Closed the door behind him.

He found us in the living room. We trembled like a falling elm tree.

Dick eased down into his chair. His cheek puffed out with his wad of chew. He rubbed his chin.

"Well now, after all these years of not paying insurance, I'm probably still ahead even after I pay for the damage."

Kenny and I exchanged nervous glances.

Dick grinned, his teeth stained from the chew. "Those damned insurance salesmen. I guess I really pulled one over on them."

Somehow, Dick was so pleased at the money he'd saved by not having insurance, he wasn't all that mad at us. "I stopped by and told the customers I'd pay for all the damages. I'm not sure what in the hell you were thinking, but I'm guessing you won't do that again."

"No sir," we said. Dick was right. Kenny eventually took over his dad's business, and I started my own tree trimming company in Omaha many years later. There's a reason you don't start sawing a tree from the bottom. Big jobs need to be taken one step at a time. The branches need to be removed, along with any dumbass teenagers from the worksite. And then you tackle the problem piece-by-piece. Turns out there are no shortcuts in the tree business.

The last time I visited town I drove by the house we smashed. It looked rough for its years. I slowed down. And there—I knew just where to look—the spot where the hole had been looked slightly different from the rest of the house. The siding never matched perfectly, but then again, neither did Kenny and I when it came to following instructions. I don't know who owns the house now, but I wondered if they ever noticed the slight difference in the siding or if they'd guessed that, once upon a time, a couple of kids brought down a tree—and a roof—in one fell timber.

WE DIDN'T START THE FIRE

The bank across the street from Harry's Conoco displayed the current time and temperature. I looked up from filling a customer's car with gas and wiped the sweat out of my eyes to make sure I could see straight. The digital numbers read 120 degrees. Our small corner of western Nebraska had turned into the devil's playground. And with half the world on fire, was it any wonder?

Half of anything depends on your starting number. In 1973, living as a high schooler in a town with a population of less than 6,000, my world at the time was pretty small. And that world burned with historical significance.

South of town by Chadron State Park near Dead Horse Road, a substantial portion of the Nebraska National Forest ignited with a hungry blaze, consuming thousands of acres. Volunteer firefighters from every town within driving distance arrived with shovels, water tanks, helicopters, and airplanes loaded with fire retardant. They fought as though battling a fire on the surface of the sun. The thirsty grass fields fueled the unstoppable flames. Though the firefighters worked around the clock, it seemed like the fire might win.

I recognized the next car in my gas line.

"Hey guys," I said, the car loaded with several friends from high school. "How many gallons do you want?"

Tim McInnis rolled his window down and popped his head out of the backseat. "Forget the gas, Don. We're gonna go fight the fire."

"Seriously?"

"Yeah, they're taking any able-bodied volunteers. Are you in?"

Something smoldered in Harry's eyes when I told him I was skipping work to go fight the fire, but I leapt in the backseat before he could yell after me.

We cracked all the windows and burned rubber down 385 South, the acrid smell of smoke thickening each mile we drew closer. "That must be it," one of us said, pointing to a ragtag group of men carrying shovels, pickaxes, and other implements. Volunteers were supposed to bring whatever tools they had, but we didn't have anything except inflated egos and shared aspirations of becoming superheroes. In hindsight, this should have been our first clue we were in over our heads.

A frazzled man in the center of the group attempted the impossible job of organizing volunteers with no idea what they were doing. Not an enviable task. Too many people were eager to help without the skills to actually be helpful.

He assigned duties like watching for traffic and being on-hand to dig ditches, but mostly people stood around helplessly as the fire raged out of sight.

One guy from town grew tired of waiting. "Let's just head up there and help," he said. Anxious to accomplish something more glamorous than watching for traffic, a bunch of us started walking up the hill. We passed a farmer who owned property west of Chadron State Park. He drove his plow in circles, overturning the vegetation on his property, a desperate attempt to starve the fire should it creep on to his farm looking for food.

We pressed on, a blaze of fervent souls climbing the hill. The wisest of the group, the men who had come most prepared, lagged behind. Wisdom, for all its goodness, also brought sore knees and overgrown bellies. Leading with brawn, rather than brains, Tim and I soon outpaced the rest of the volunteers and reached the top of the ridge far ahead of everyone else.

From our viewpoint, we could see planes swooping down, dropping streams of reddish-orange fire retardant. The sky looked dark, filled with black ominous clouds that didn't hold a drop of rain. Without a watch, you'd be hard pressed to tell afternoon from dinnertime.

"Hold up there!" the men called after us. We looked down at the guys struggling for breath as they made the final ascent. The smoky air combined with clogged arteries made this a difficult climb for them. They kept calling at us to stop, the way wisdom pleads with folly.

"Well heck," Tim said. "We'll never get there if we have

to wait for those old fogies."

"I'm not stopping," I said. "We're not going to run away from it."

We ignored the calls of prudence. If a burning bush spoke to us, we wouldn't have listened to it either. We hiked down a small incline before ascending an even higher hill. That's when we felt the heat. "What should we do now?" I yelled.

Before Tim could respond, we witnessed something I'd never seen before or since. Deer, porcupines, rabbits, and raccoons ran down the hill towards us, away from the fire. Heedless of our proximity, they swerved around us, unafraid for once of human presence, solely focused on survival.

With even a fraction of today's wisdom, I might've recognized the stupidity in running toward the fire; but being young and dumb, and having already left wisdom lagging on the hill behind us, we looked at each other and said, "Cool."

And then we kept walking.

We climbed the next ridge, and in the valley below we saw three hotshot crews. Each of the professional firefighters was outfitted with a helmet, heavy protective clothing, and sophisticated equipment. I looked down at my sweat-stained Harry's Conoco T-shirt and blue jeans. We hiked down the embankment and approached the fire fighters.

"Holy crap, what are you two doing out here?"

We'd been spotted. A firefighter approached us, his yellow jacket nearly brown from dirt and ash. "We're volunteers," Tim said.

The man's skeptical look was a little insulting. "You kids can't be down here." He turned and shouted to a group working behind him. "Hey, we gotta get these kids out of here!"

By now, darkness quickly descended, making it too late in the day to take wayward teens back to safety. These hotshot teams didn't need one more logistical nightmare. Instead, another guy handed Tim and I a hard hat and a bright colored vest and told us to hop in the back of a nearby pickup.

"Stay there and do not move. Do you understand?"

We nodded, a little dumbstruck.

Some might have thought we'd wandered into one of the circles of hell. There we were, two ill-prepared teenage boys sitting in the back of a pickup truck surrounded by busy firefighters and facing an oncoming fire of epic proportions. But for us, we'd reached seventh heaven. We looked at each other and exchanged stupid grins. Could we do anything cooler than what we were doing?

Our heads swiveled back and forth as though we were watching a tennis match. In one quadrant of the scene, crews talked on radio to helicopters and airplanes, calling in locations and communicating important information over the static. In another area, workers set out flagging tape, marking firelines and ditches. To the right, we watched hotshots run burnout operations, intentionally lighting fires to meet the oncoming flames. The higher the fires climbed on the hill, the faster they went. For every ten degrees of slope, the fire doubled its speed. We didn't need to sit in a classroom to learn the physics of heat transfer and airflow dynamics. We were immersed in an unfilmed documentary, and the images burned into our minds. Another group of men used shovels and pickaxes, digging pre-marked ditches.

"Hey Tim," I said.

"Yeah?"

"Look at all these shovels."

Pickaxes, shovels, and other equipment filled the back of the pickup. Tim and I didn't know anything about communicating directions over the radio or marking firelines, but we were good Nebraska boys. We knew shovels and dirt.

The gleam in Tim's eyes told me everything I needed to know. He was on board. "Alright," I said, "let's start digging."

I jumped out of the truck bed, stopping only to grab a shovel. Walking up the side of the hill in my hard hat, jeans, and vest, I imagined myself to be hot stuff, and not only because I could taste the ash which fell in dandruff-like flakes from the sky. My eyes watered from smoke and the back of my throat tickled, but I wouldn't have traded this for an afternoon of pumping gas at Harry's.

Tim had a pickaxe in-hand and joined a row of men. We worked steadily with rivulets of sweat streaking black lines down our smoke and dirt-covered faces.

Soon, we heard cussing. "Hey, I told you kids to stay in that pickup!"

We'd been caught. After giving us a thorough verbal thrashing, the fireman wandered off, and one of the other diggers looked back at us. "Don't worry about him. Keep doing what you're doing, but make sure you stay behind me."

"Yes, sir!"

The shovels continued in steady rhythm until the only light remaining came from the defensive firelines and distant flames. Darkness encompassed the entire sky, erasing even the stars. Clouds of ash devoured the moon and any light it might have given. We were alone with the darkness and one of the biggest fires in the history of western Nebraska.

Crews set up camp, which consisted of simple safety blankets for shut-eye in between watch shifts. At that point, there was no way for Tim and I to return to the volunteer station, and unbeknownst to us, all the volunteers had been sent back to town for the night. Camping with the hotshot crews was our only choice, whether we liked it or not. And we liked it.

For the next two nights and three days, Tim and I spent every waking moment with shovels and pickaxes in our hands. When we weren't digging, we were sent to fetch tools. We filled water canteens, worked as errand boys and messengers, living out a little boy fantasy camp. We were having a blast.

Looking back, I wonder what the hotshots truly thought of a couple of over-eager kids playacting as firemen. But we were too caught up in the moment to care. Where they saw life and death, we saw adventure.

You'd think there'd have been a feeling of elation when news came announcing the fire was contained. But all I felt was deflated. No more ditches to dig. No more water canteens to refill. We looked like the dregs of a burnt-out campfire. Our clothes stuck to our bodies, blackened beyond recognition. Layers of soot on our faces made it impossible to tell whether we were 16 or 60. We missed our ride home by two days and since we were so far out in the country, we loaded up into the firetrucks. My sadness grew as I watched the blackened grass and broken trees become smaller out the window. I wanted nothing more than to stay and fight fires for the rest of my life.

Not once had we thought to contact our parents. Had it crossed our minds, we would have been out of luck, because cell phones didn't exist. No search parties came looking for us. In fact, no one seemed all that worried at all.

When I walked in the front door, my mom wasn't too concerned, though she told me to make sure my clothes went straight in the wash. "Harry said you headed out there. I figured you were out there doing some good," was all she said.

When I returned to work the next day, Harry said something to the tune of, "I suppose that was more fun than working here." He didn't know the half of it.

If two teenage boys went missing during a wildfire today, there'd be nothing else on the news channels. But I can remember how unconcerned everybody was. Our world had been on fire, and someone had to do something about it. Why not us? Sure, it started out as an adventure. Dirt needed shoveled, and we could shovel it. We weren't going to complain that it wasn't our job.

Maybe that's what we've lost today. The willingness to get our hands dirty, to face the fire head-on. We've made a big mess of this world and there's a whole lot of cleanup work, but not too many people are willing to grab a shovel. Sometimes you have to fight, even when it's not your fire to put out. During the Dead Horse Fire, neither Tim nor I ever stopped to point fingers or cast blame on whatever caused the fire in the first place. The fire was there and needed putting out. There wasn't more to it.

Several months later I was back at Harry's Conoco and the bank across the street only registered double digits. Tim pulled up in his car, and I asked him how much gas he wanted.

"No gas," he said. "I was stopping by to see if you'd seen the newspaper."

"Can't say I have."

"There's an article that says whoever volunteered during the fire can come down to the station and fill out a form and there's a fund to pay the volunteers."

"No kidding?"

"Dead serious. What time do you get off?"

I looked at the clock on the bank. "In about twenty minutes."

"I'll just wait for you and we can go down to the station together."

Being broke-ass high school kids, we were eager to fill

out those forms. I slipped out of work five minutes early and went straight to the station. We had to include the location where we served and the number of hours worked. Since money was involved, I made sure my handwriting was legible. We handed them the paperwork, and they handed us a check for $173, which was more money than God had at the time. We couldn't believe our good fortune. We were rich, and all because we'd been too dumb to know if all of God's creatures were running away from the fire, we should turn around and run too.

Tim and I shared a guilty grin as we pocketed the check. It felt like we'd pulled off a heist. Sure, the money felt good, but nothing compared to those three days in the ash and smoke. As we left the station, I could still feel the weight of that shovel in my hands, the heat of the fire on my face. I think Tim and I both would have paid good money for those experiences, but we'd stumbled into double fortune. In addition to the experience and paycheck, we carried a new-found sense of pride.

We didn't start the fire, but we sure as hell helped put it out.

NOT SO GREAT EXPECTATIONS

A father's expectations are not a light burden to carry.
Or so I've heard.

The oldest son of a single mom, I didn't have any great expectations. This is not to say there were no expectations. They just weren't great.

My only concept of a father's expectations of a son came in the form of observation. It wasn't uncommon in my day for a child to follow in his parent's footsteps. Estimates suggest as many as 50 percent of individuals pursued similar career paths as their parents in the 1970s, especially in industries like farming, manufacturing, and family-run businesses.

Since my dad set the family legacy at an extremely low bar, I had no interest in carrying on his torch of alcoholism and family abandonment. My sights were higher—all the way to the sky.

The nuns at Chadron Catholic School expected I'd make

very little out of myself. They told my mom time and again I wasn't cut out to be an academic. With my dominant left hand tied behind my back like some outlaw caught in the act, I was forced to write with my right. My reward? A ruler across the knuckles. When I predicted that one day machines would spell on my behalf, no amount of prayers could keep me from my punishment.

Mom expected I wouldn't succeed intellectually beyond high school and discouraged my college ambitions. "Donald, why would you go to college when you have a perfectly good job?"

"Which job?" At the time I had several.

"Harry's Conoco."

"I get paid to fill people's cars with gas and to wash their windshields. I don't really see myself doing that for the rest of my life."

"It's a stepping stone," she said. "Someday he could turn over the whole business to you."

Harry Lliteras was my uncle, and it was a well-known fact that none of his kids had any intention to take over the family business. Perhaps my mom felt guilty because there was no family business for me to take over.

"I just don't see myself owning a gas station. I want to be a pilot."

"Can't you be a pilot without going to college?"

"To fly the big airlines, you have to have a four-year degree."

Mom didn't say much after that. Being a strong Catholic, she couldn't disregard the nuns' comments about my apparent lack of brain cells. If the nuns declared me a dunce, that was practically divine decree. Who was she to question the wisdom of the Almighty? Unfortunately, my high school grades weren't much of an argument in my defense. But I had better things to do than study and go to class.

Jim Strang managed the fixed-base operator—the FBO—out of the Chadron Airport, which handled everything from fueling to flight training, and I worked for him throughout high school. His son, Gordon, was a year younger than me and knew all about a father's expectations. At a young age, Gordon already had his private pilot license and was working on his A&P mechanic license. Gordon had a keen mind and a lot going for him. But he didn't want to be a pilot. He wanted to be an electrical engineer.

Of course, Jim, like any concerned parent, wanted the best for Gordon. And he was convinced the best for Gordon was to fly airplanes.

One day in school, Gordon cornered me in the hallway. "Dad's giving me the Cessna 210. Any time it's not being used, we can fly it wherever we want."

I'd never heard more beautiful words. Any guy can invite a girl to the drive-in or to go for a cruise down Third Street, but if you really want to score points with a pretty girl, you offer her the world with a 310 horsepower engine. It was the ultimate high school fantasy: unlimited access to a plane, a pocketful of Jim's credit, and an aerial view of towns where we'd never have to face the same girl twice.

Gordon had no interest in manning the pilot's seat. Instead, he treated the cockpit like a fancy limo. I was the driver. He was the in-flight entertainment for all the ladies. This was fine by me because, truth be told, my interest in flying far exceeded the idea of high school romance.

We touched down in all the surrounding states—visiting North Dakota, flying into Helena, Montana, making several landings in Denver, Colorado. It was easy enough to sit in the captain's seat and imagine the 210 was mine.

Jim approached me one day as I cleaned bugs off the plane. He had a big grin on his face. "I'm really proud of Gordon," he said.

"Oh yeah?" I offered a return smile unsure of where this conversation was headed.

"He's already put twenty-two hours on this plane." He placed his hand against the 210's smooth, white nose.

"You don't say," I said, scrubbing faster.

"I'm really excited to see his logbook."

I nodded, swallowing hard. *Oh geez,* I thought, *I bet Gordon didn't think to enter anything into his logbook.*

I felt kinda bad for Gordon. His dad pushed him in a direction he didn't want to go. What if my dad had been a pilot? Would I have still dreamed of soaring into the clouds? Or would I have wanted to own a gas station instead? Perhaps I was better off not knowing a father's expectations.

A few weeks later Jim needed to fly the 210 somewhere; instead of piloting it himself, he thought it would be the perfect father-son bonding opportunity. "Come on, Gordon," he said. "Show me what you've got."

Gordon had no choice. He climbed on board and squirmed into the pilot's seat. I wasn't there to see exactly what happened, but I do know Gordon did not fly the 210 that day.

The next time Jim saw me, there was nothing resembling a grin on his face. "I bet you feel pretty comfortable in this plane, don't you," he said.

"I don't know what you mean."

"The 210," he said, gesticulating towards the plane as though it wasn't parked right in front of us. "You've logged a lot of hours over the past few months."

"Sorry, sir. I don't know what you are talking about."

"Cut the bullshit," Jim said. "I know you've been the one flying it. Gordon didn't even know how to turn the thing on. And when I checked his logbook, I didn't see a single mention of the 210."

I'd been caught. Our days of cruising with the 210 were over.

But I went to college and graduated. I even became an airline pilot. Looking back, I can see the protective nature in my mom's low expectations for me. From her viewpoint, she thought a grounded job like working in a gas station would provide stability; whereas, a life in the sky would always have gravity threatening to bring me down. Mom thought by dampening my expectations, I wouldn't have as far to fall.

Years later, as I watched my daughter and son take their first wobbly steps, I gained a new understanding of parental aspirations. Holding them in my arms, I realized the weight of expectations could either uplift them or hold them back. My children would face their ambitions, both from others and from themselves. But I vowed to give them the freedom to forge their own paths, free from the burdens of external pressures.

I shouldn't have worried. My determined and stubborn children knew what they wanted from life at a very young age, and like me, they simply shrugged off the weight of unwanted projections. Fortunately, my kids turned out just fine. And neither of them ever tried to convince me to invest in a gas station. The greatest gift I offered my children was my support, allowing them to take flight, unburdened by expectations that were not their own.

A DIAMOND IN THE ROUGH

When I started at Chadron State College, I had one goal: get a degree—any degree—so I could fly for the airlines. Back then, the FAA didn't care if your diploma was in aviation or origami, so long as it qualified as a four-year degree. Since CSC didn't offer aviation or origami, I spent my first couple years bouncing between classes like a pinball, hoping something would stick.

Journalism seemed like a good fit. I liked writing, and my time at the local radio station gave me on-the-job training. I enrolled in my first news writing class. Each week we dug up stories of interest on campus, conducted the necessary interviews, wrote it up, and turned it in for editing. Our professor, Mr. Donahue, marked up our work, and we revised our final copies for a grade.

While I graduated high school by my hangnails, I aimed higher for college. For the most part, my report cards looked good enough to hang on the fridge. I carried a solid *B* in news writing, which wasn't a point of shame. But Mr. Donahue issued a challenge at the beginning of the year. "As," Mr. Donahue warned us, "will only be given to students whose work is published in *The Eagle Newspaper*."

He'd thrown down the gauntlet. I picked it up.

But by mid-semester, with me still clutching this gauntlet, worry trickled in. So far Mr. Donahue hadn't selected a single one of my articles for publication. Frustration simmered. Once we turned the stories in, fate took control. Fate was a four-letter word I didn't need in my life. I wanted control. I wanted an *A*. I needed a story published.

Meanwhile on the music scene, Neil Diamond published one of his songs about every ten minutes. You couldn't listen to the radio without hearing one. During an afternoon daydream, while "Sweet Caroline" played in the background, I had an epiphany—Neil Diamond had a wife, or at least I assumed. I wasn't the type to follow celebrity gossip.

But what if she wanted a normal life? What if, tired of the limelight, she decided to go to college? A small, unassuming school in the middle of nowhere—like Chadron State.

And what if I was the only one who knew?

I grabbed my pen.

I scribbled notes.

I wrote until the pen ran out of ink.

*

"C'mon, Osborn. You gotta tell me who she is."

"She's that quiet brunette in the front row of biology,

124

isn't she?"

"I'll give you a hundred bucks."

"You can borrow my car."

"My girlfriend says she'll kiss you."

My story became the center of discussion during our next class. Everyone surrounded my desk, begging for me to give away the identity of Neil Diamond's wife.

"No way, guys, it would ruin her life," I said. "That's literally why she picked Chadron, because she could hide in plain sight here. She's been here for a couple of years, and no one has figured out who she is. I'm certainly not going to be the one to blow it for her."

"We should form an investigation squad," someone suggested.

"Why would she tell a bozo like you all this stuff?" asked one of my friends.

"Look guys, I can't tell you more than what's in the article. It would be unethical for me to accept bribery. Let's treat her like we'd want to be treated in this situation," I said. "She may be famous, but she has feelings and wants to be treated like a regular person."

No one could do a quick Google search. Fact checking would require tracking down old periodicals or searching microfiche for interviews with Neil Diamond. Besides, believing proved more interesting.

Mr. Donohue read my story with one eyebrow raised. "Interesting," he said, tapping his pen against the paper. "Your lead is well written."

"Thank you."

"You're telling me Neil Diamond's wife is attending Chadron State?"

"According to my source," I said.

"What have I taught you about sources?"

I searched my memory for something useful. "We should always have more than one?"

"Yes," Mr. Donohue said. "And why?"

"Because one source could get it wrong?"

"Exactly. You need at least a second source to corroborate that information. Better yet, you should have three sources."

"But you also said a good newsman won't give up his source if they don't want to be named," I countered.

He exhaled, rubbing his temple. "You understand what happens if we publish something like this and it turns out to be false?"

I shrugged. As long as I got an *A*, other repercussions didn't concern me.

"Okay, I'll publish this one," Mr. Donahue said. "But since you don't name your source, we have to call it 'Fact or Fiction.' Otherwise it goes against everything I've taught you."

"Yes, sir," I said, already picturing a fat, beautiful *A*.

*

The article made me more famous than Neil Diamond's wife. I couldn't walk across campus without being hounded. "Please, tell us who she is," students begged.

"I'll buy you lunch!"

"Wanna ride my motorcycle?"

"The beers will be on me!"

People cornered me after class.

I couldn't find a quiet place in the library to study. "This is exactly why Neil Diamond's wife went incognito," I confessed to a sympathetic friend.

Girls with even a hint of mystery found themselves under suspicion. Some leaned into it—walking the campus in oversized sunglasses, sighing wistfully at the mention of Neil Diamond. Others weren't as lucky. I overheard one girl pleading, "For the last time, my dad sells tractors in North Platte. I am NOT Neil Diamond's wife."

But attention spans are shorter than Neil Diamond's first marriage. Articles read one week become the lining in a parakeet's cage the next, so my celebrity status faded fast.

In the end, Neil Diamond's wife collected her diploma and disappeared—just as mysteriously as she arrived.

As for me? I ditched journalism for criminal justice but walked away with two things: an *A* in news writing and a campus full of people who believed I had the inside scoop on a woman who never existed.

ANNIE AT SPAGHETTI WORKS

My favorite human pet was coming to visit for the weekend, and I kept looking out the window to see if the car had arrived. Newly married with no kids of our own, I wanted to impress Beth with my language skills. I'd always been fluent in two languages: Dog and Kid. I could get by in English, but I thrived with canines and miniature humans.

"Any sign of them?" Beth called from the kitchen.

"Not yet."

My youngest sister, Annie, came into the world the same month I graduated from college. Though a scrawny thing, I loved playing with her. As a three-year-old, she wasn't yet smart enough to realize I couldn't actually pull off her ear, swallow it, and puke it back into my hand before returning it to the side of her head. Only kids could appreciate true comedic genius.

Beth and I were anxious to have miniature humans of our own. And if my relationship with my baby sister was any indication, I'd be named *Father of the Year* without much effort. Beth and I had talked over every aspect of parenting and wouldn't repeat any of the mistakes our own parents had made. For one thing, we were already into our mid-twenties. My mom had me at nineteen, so we'd already gained a lot more life experience than she'd had starting out. We had a stable marriage, which was a big improvement from my own childhood home.

Much of my childhood development knowledge existed in the theoretical realm at this point. But I'd observed plenty of examples of poor parenting in the airports, and it didn't seem too difficult to simply do the opposite. I could stop a kid from crying with a single goofy face. I was the Peter Pan amongst the Big People. I never wanted to grow up. I vowed to never be one of those boring adults who'd forgotten how to have fun.

I looked at my watch. They should have been here by now. Knowing Mom, they'd have been on the road by 6 a.m., and the drive took seven and a half hours at most. Assuming they'd stopped for gas and lunch along the way, and accounting for the time change between Chadron and Omaha, I figured they'd get here by 2 p.m. at the latest. The clock read 2:15.

I started to worry around 2:45, but as I'd paced by the window for the dozenth time, my stepdad pulled onto the street in front of our house. "They're here!" I called, rushing outside.

From the moment I saw my mom, I worried they'd driven through a tornado on the way here. She looked uptight and unhappy. She clutched at her purse in a way that indicated she needed a cigarette first and foremost. My stepdad, Earl, asked her to stop smoking when they found out she was pregnant with my youngest sister. Though she resumed the habit as soon as the baby dropped into the doctor's arms, she maintained a level of secrecy about her vice. She kept her smoking relegated to the upstairs bathroom in their Chadron house, blowing the smoke out the open window like a guilty teenager.

"I'm just going to stretch my legs," she said in greeting and headed straight to our backyard, her purse already halfway open.

Annie tumbled out of the car, looking disheveled, her hair in stringy tangles, but with a smile plastered on her face. "Donald!" she screamed, running straight into my arms.

Earl took his time getting out. He didn't do anything in a hurry. "How was the drive?" I asked him, shaking his hand.

"Oh, it was pretty good," he said.

"Did Mom have you in the car by 6 a.m.?" I asked.

"Four," Earl said.

"In the morning?"

"She wanted to beat the traffic."

The only possible traffic on a Nebraska highway at 4 a.m. would be a family of skunks crossing the road. "Did you stop a bunch of times?" I asked, trying to understand the discrepancy between their starting and arrival time.

"Once for gas and once for lunch," Earl said.

My mind attempted the calculations. I remembered driving with Earl on previous occasions. He liked to keep the speedometer five miles below the speed limit. Still, the hours didn't add up. "Did you find our house okay?"

"That was a little tricky," he admitted. "It took us a couple of hours to find the right street, but we figured it out."

No wonder Mom looked like she'd passed through a storm. She'd been without a cigarette since 4 a.m. and then they'd driven the streets of Omaha for two solid hours. I could picture them pulled over in a sketchy neighborhood, Mom locking all the doors, cussing at Earl, while he methodically consulted the atlas spread over the steering wheel.

"Well, come on in," I said.

Earl and I each grabbed a suitcase. Beth welcomed us inside and Annie greeted her suspiciously. I remembered one of the first times I brought Beth home to meet my family. Annie had popped up between us and possessively extricated Beth's hand from my own, claiming territory over me.

"Are you sure she isn't your kid?" Beth grilled me later.

Mom came through the front door, smoke clinging to her clothes. She still looked nervous, but the desperation had left her eyes. She took a seat next to Earl on the couch. "Nice to see you, Beth," she said. "Your house sure looks nice."

"Why thank you, Loretta."

We sat formally in the living room, while Annie crawled around on her hands and knees with our dogs, Bandit and

Buddy. "Does she need to be taken out?" Beth asked.

"Anna Marie, you are going to ruin your knees," Mom said.

"So she still likes to pretend she's a dog?" I asked.

"She barked at the meter reader just last week," Mom said.

"Well, she's got an imagination, that's for sure." Beth chuckled nervously.

"Hey," I said. "I bet I can teach her how to fetch."

While the adults made small talk, I found one of the dog toys and threw it down the hallway. "Annie, fetch!" Dutifully, she bounded away, bringing the toy back in her mouth, dropping it obediently by my feet. I embraced the moment of pride. "Good dog," I said, patting her sandy blonde hair. Her smile stretched across her freckled face. She still had perfect, tiny baby teeth, and she let me see all of them.

Earl started asking me about different businesses in Omaha, especially the ones he'd frequented when he'd been buying parts for his business, *Henkens Implement*. The tractor company had some acclaim in western Nebraska as one of the top tractor businesses, dealing mainly in Allis-Chalmers. Earl, a renowned mechanic, could fix about anything. He'd even been known to fly parts to farmers in his Piper Cub airplane, landing directly in their fields.

"I used to come to Omaha every so often," Earl was saying. "I'd sure like to see some of those old buildings."

"Well you know," I said, inspired. "Those are all in an area they now call *Old Market*. They've turned it into this shopping center with all these little businesses, and my favorite restaurant is in that part of town. We should go."

I didn't stop to consider our visitors had been driving since 4 a.m., but they were too polite to argue. We arrived at the Old Market and spent a few hours walking around, wandering through stores, looking at things. At first Annie dashed around the sidewalk like some sort of spastic rabid squirrel, but she was starting to wilt. I popped her up on my shoulders. "You're a horsie," she said. "Yee haw!"

"I'm getting hungry," I said. "Should we gallop to Spaghetti Works? It's just around the corner."

Everyone agreed and I bounced along happily, completely in my element. Annie laughed with delight and glee as her brain knocked against the inside of her skull. I bucked like a bronco, and she was Annie Oakley of the wild west. Mom remained quiet, clutching her purse tightly and keeping close watch over her surroundings. She didn't like the city.

We entered the restaurant. "Table for five," I said.

The hostess led us to a table.

"I want to sit by Donald," Annie said.

"Alright, you can sit right here." I patted the booth beside me, and she snuggled in close. "Do you like Spaghetti?"

"Yes."

"She likes plain spaghetti," Mom elaborated, "with nothing on top."

"They can do spaghetti any way you like here," I said. "They can do any topping and any pasta. And there's a salad bar too."

Annie refused the salad bar. "I don't like vegetables."

"Horses eat carrots," I countered.

"You're the horse," she said. "You can eat mine."

I kept Annie entertained while we waited for dinner to arrive. At one point I bit off my own thumb before making it magically reappear behind her head. She whipped around, looking behind her, trying to figure out the trick. "Good pet," I said, tickling her belly until she giggled.

"Here's our food," Beth announced. The waitress approached carrying steaming plates, laden with fresh pasta, each soaking in its own ocean of delicious sauce.

"And this one is for you," the waitress said. She placed a smaller plate in front of my sister, plain spaghetti topped with a small cube of butter.

We thanked the waitress. My stomach growled. I started twisting the noodles around my fork, anticipating the first bite, my mouth filling with salivary excitement.

That's when it started.

Annie screamed with more ferocity than those of the unlucky souls who were once thrown to the lions in ancient Roman colosseums.

"Did she burn herself?" Beth asked, concerned.

"Anna Marie, stop screaming," Mom said.

I made a silly face. I patted the top of her head. Was now a good time to pretend to eat her nose? Her screams only increased in volume. Her face twisted into such wild abandon I seriously worried she might bite me.

The waitress returned to our table, frantic. "Is everything okay?"

No lady, nothing is okay.

"It's the pasta," Mom shouted over the noise. "She wanted plain pasta and this one had butter on it."

"Oh, I'm so sorry. I'll get her a new plate right away." The waitress sprinted off as though being chased by a lion.

The screams continued in earnest.

"Seriously?" I said. "All this because of a tablespoon of butter?"

Beth sent me a pleading look. I could hear her voice in my head. *Okay Donald, I thought you could speak Kid fluently. Now would be a good time to start speaking!* She plastered a pained smile on her face.

"Look, a horse!" I pointed. "A doggy riding a bicycle! Have you heard the one about the guy who walked in a bar?" I could have been speaking in tongues, but nothing could penetrate the misery of this one small girl.

I've never seen a demon possession, and until that day I'm not even sure my theological beliefs aligned with the idea, but I became a believer. This was the tantrum of all tantrums. Every eye in the restaurant turned in our direction. Nothing worked. We forked pasta into our mouths, attempting normalcy. We consoled. We promised ice cream. If I'd had a tranquilizer injection, nothing could have stopped me from using it.

The waitress brought out a new plate of pasta, absent of any offensive butter. Annie wouldn't even look at it. At this point, she lapsed into full convulsions. Had there been a contest for most extensive tantrum, there'd have been no question who won. "Can I bring you boxes?" the waitress asked, noting our barely touched plates.

"No," Mom said. "I just want to get out of here."

We carried the little monster kicking and screaming to the car. Since this was before car seats, I sort of shoved her in the backseat between Mom and Earl. As I drove, she continued to flail about, kicking the backs of our seats, wetting the leather with her snot and tears.

"Should we pull over?" Beth asked. "Maybe find a garden hose and spray her down? I think she's having an aneurysm."

I drove in a blind rage. It wasn't a long drive, but it felt like we'd covered the distance between Chadron and Omaha. My little pet's sudden case of canine distemper threw me for a loop. The child was obviously broken. None of my tried-and-true tricks worked. The screams didn't stop until Annie passed out in the bed we'd prepared, her face still red and scrunched as though even in sleep the demons threatened peace.

"Is anyone hungry?" Beth asked, when we finally sunk back into the quiet of the living room.

"I'm just going to step outside for a minute," Mom said, grabbing her purse on the way out the door.

I sure as hell wished I smoked. In that moment, I'd have given anything for a nicotine addiction. I caught Beth's gaze from across the room, and we shared a small smile, knowing a child of ours would never make such a scene.

From that moment onward, it became known as the Spaghetti Works Incident. To this day, I bet the waitress or anyone else who'd been in the near vicinity still tells the story of the night a little blonde girl terrorized an entire restaurant.

Shortly after Mom returned, the rest of us went to bed. No one had the energy or will to speak or make direct eye contact.

When I awoke the next morning, I immediately felt unsettled, scared to be in my own home. What horrors might await me today?

Mom greeted me in the kitchen, a hot mug of black coffee in front of her. And there sat Annie, eating a bowl of Cheerios. They weren't plain Cheerios, but she didn't eat them with milk and sugar like most kids. Instead she ate them in the Osborn way—with a tablespoon of butter melted over the top and salted generously. *Sure, now she liked butter.* As soon as she saw me, she sat down her spoon and buried her face in the bowl. "Look, Donald! I'm eating my dog food!"

"Anna Marie!" Mom chided.

But I just smiled and pet her head. "Should I put your bowl on the floor so you can eat like a real dog?"

"Donald!" Mom said.

But Annie barked and was down on her hands and knees ready to finish her breakfast.

Beth and Earl appeared in the kitchen sometime later, both wearing equally traumatized expressions. But Annie was in the happiest of moods, a *cute what did I do?* expression on her face. For the rest of the day she was sweet and cheerful and she performed all of her tricks admirably.

*

"Okay, for one moment did you stop to think I was probably exhausted from having been up since 4 a.m.? And did you think about the fact I'd been in a car for ten hours and then you drug me all over Old Market and then expected me to behave in a restaurant? I was three!" Annie says defensively.

I'm still telling this story more than forty years later, but now my baby sister acts all high and mighty like maybe I didn't fully understand toddlers when I was twenty-six years-old.

"Do you think about that story differently now that you've had your own children?" Annie asks me.

"My own kids never threw tantrums," I say. "At least not like the one you threw in Spaghetti Works."

"That is such bull," Annie says. "But I wanna know, how would you have reacted differently to that situation now that you've had kids?"

"Great question," I say. "I think I would have said, 'Piss on her. Just let her scream and cry on the floor. She'll tire herself out eventually.' And then I would have eaten that plate of pasta."

"Donald," Annie says. "You are impossible."

"I don't think I could take you to Spaghetti Works even now," I say. "I'm afraid the waitress might still be working there and she'd recognize you and have a heart attack."

"Oh please," Annie says, and I hear the click clack of her keyboard as she types my words into her computer. I can't hear her roll her eyes, but I can see it, even though we are only talking on the phone.

But I know she'll type the story, even though it'll make her look ridiculous and now everyone will know she used to pretend she was a dog, even past the time it was probably age appropriate. I know this, because she's a good pet. I trained her well.

WITH GREAT GENIUS

"Katie, hurry up. You're going to make us late again," Rob called to his big sister.

"What do I care if we're late?" Katie said, tossing her backpack in the car. "It's not like they're going to start without me. I'm smarter than the teacher. She needs me to help teach the math lesson."

"You are not smarter than the teacher," Rob said.

"Wanna bet?"

Rob knew better than to bet against his sister.

Katie took his silence as victory. "I'm the smartest person in my class. I'm always the first to turn in my tests, I win all the mad minutes, and I corrected three of my teacher's mistakes this week alone."

"Oh yeah?" Rob smirked. "If you're so smart, why did you forget your shoes at home?"

Katie looked down at her stockinged-feet in horror. "We need to turn around!" she screeched.

"Great," Rob grumbled. "Now we're really going to be late."

*

From the moment my daughter was born, I knew she was special. She arrived on Katie-time, meaning when she was ready and to hell with the rest of the world. And when she finally made her appearance, I'd never heard a creature scream at the level and length she managed in the first moments of her life. Forget breaking glass. Katie's screams could break diamonds.

I learned in a Psychology class about a child's early ability to manipulate their parents. For infants, this ability is a survival technique. The baby cries to be fed, to be changed, to indicate sleepiness. Without those pitiful screams, babies couldn't communicate their needs.

Katie mastered the art of manipulation faster than most. One of my earliest parenting mistakes—right up there with teaching her to talk—was rocking her to sleep in an old wooden antique rocking chair. It was soothing, relaxing, and frankly, I enjoyed it as much as she did.

Little did I know I was conditioning her like a tiny, screaming Pavlovian experiment. The moment I tried to transfer her to the crib? Instant meltdown. Not a normal baby fuss, but a full-scale protest, as if I'd just thrown her into solitary confinement. I swear, she could have organized a hunger strike if she hadn't been so well-fed.

Eventually, I realized the truth: I wasn't rocking her to sleep—she was rocking me into submission.

Katie's questions came earlier and with more intensity than

other kids her age. "There's no way Santa Claus could be real," she told me at the ripe old age of four. "Nobody could do that in one night," and "Oh for goodness sakes, now you're telling me a giant bunny goes around and hides eggs at Easter?"

We didn't even attempt to introduce the Tooth Fairy.

Katie really caught me off-guard when she asked me the most dreaded of all parenting questions. "Where do babies come from?"

Normally, I'd have been unprepared for such a question, but I'd just read a parenting book that talked about answering kids' questions as honestly as possible. No need to go into detail, of course, but it was better for parents to be the source of information. If the child wants to know more, allow them to ask the questions.

Well, Katie's questions started and didn't end. Her incredible mind wouldn't quit asking questions until she knew everything. Her eyes grew big and my face turned red.

"So, where do you guys do this?" she asked.

It took me a moment to respond. "Usually in the bed."

"Yuck," she said. "I used to sleep in that bed."

Mercifully, the conversation ended.

I called my mom one day. "You sure had it easy raising kids," I told her.

"Oh, I'm sure," she said, no doubt remembering things much differently.

"You have no idea how hard it is to raise a budding genius."

"That's true," she said. "You were pretty easy to raise."

For Katie, school was like a game of checkers—straightforward, easy, and something she could win without much effort. Meanwhile, everyone else seemed to be playing chess, struggling to think five moves ahead while she had already jumped across the board and declared victory.

One teacher even described her as "scary smart."

One would think Katie's intelligence was a blessed gift. But with great genius, comes a great lack of responsibility.

I remember one day standing around the kitchen listening to her brag about being the first member of our family to have a master's degree. Minutes later I delivered a can of gas to her, because she was stranded on the side of the interstate with only her one-hundred-fifty-pound Newfoundland, Charlie, as roadside assistance. Turns out, geniuses don't waste brainpower on things like fuel gauges.

My idea of being on time means I leave early enough to have a flat tire and still arrive at my destination fifteen minutes early. Katie-time means getting there just in time to grab the landing gear—probably without shoes.

This might be a slight exaggeration. Katie usually boards the third flight of the day, even though she was scheduled for the first.

Other things Katie has been late for: her own wedding, her brother's wedding, every appointment she's ever had.

But, as Katie herself would point out, she's someone worth waiting for. She's collected advanced degrees faster than I can collect pocket lint. It would take a whole book to list her accomplishments, but I've watched her work a classroom of college students, counsel people I might have deemed beyond help, and argue with people with strong beliefs to the point they just give up and say, "Okay, I think like you think now," before running screaming to the airport or into the woods to hide.

Recently, she was interviewed on ABC's *20/20* news show explaining how a convicted criminal in prison couldn't possibly be guilty. Now she's co-hosting the *Trial and Error* podcast. Part of the fun of being her dad is waiting to see what she'll come up with next.

Heck, I wouldn't be surprised if she ended up as leader of the free world someday—if she could only get to the campaign trail on time.

DOLLAR STORE DEBACLE

"Here's the deal," I said. "You can go in and each pick out one item—anything you want."

"Anything?" Katie said.

"Anything." I pulled two crisp dollar bills out of my hand, along with some change to cover the tax. "I'll be waiting right out here. Make sure you look after your brother."

"No problem. Let's go, Rob."

I watched my kids as they walked into the store. The door jangled as it opened and closed. Spotting a bench in the shade, I took a seat. Then I proceeded to compliment myself on being a parenting genius.

Dollar Stores were brand new to Omaha. I had kid-duty all day and I'd run out of ideas to keep them entertained. We'd been driving past the new store when overcome by my own brilliance.

Katie was a careful shopper. It would take her forever to go up and down each aisle to make her selection. Rob wouldn't go too far from his sister. They'd be as happy as Christmas morning, I'd get some peace and quiet, and it would only cost me two bucks. No doubt my *Father of the Year* certificate would be waiting for me in the mailbox when I got home.

Almost an hour passed before I heard the door jangle again. Katie burst out, clutching her purchase and grinning like a gambler with an ace up her sleeve. Rob toddled behind.

"Thank you, Daddy," Katie said, all sugar and spice.

On the ride home, Katie chatted happily about every thought which entered her head. Rob stayed quiet. This wasn't unusual. Of the two kids, Rob tended to keep his thoughts close. But his quiet had me worried. "Are you okay, Rob Bob?"

That's when he started to cry.

"What's wrong?"

In the rear-view mirror I could see tears run down his cheeks.

"I didn't want to buy this," he said, holding up his Dollar Store purchase. "Katie made me."

I looked at Katie. "Is that true?"

"I didn't make him," she said, crossing her arms in front of her chest. "I just told him it was way cooler than what he wanted to buy."

"Katie said the thing I picked out was stupid," Rob howled.

"Well, it was." Katie shrugged. "If you don't want what you bought, Rob, I'll have it."

He tossed it up to her in the front seat. "I don't want it."

"Suits me," she said.

I saw exactly what had transpired in the Dollar Store. Katie had wanted two toys, and she'd figured out how to manipulate her little brother into picking out what she wanted. Even at a young age, Katie no doubt had the highest IQ in our family. It was actually a little frightening.

"Katie, that was very naughty," I scolded. "Listen, the next time we go to the Dollar Store, Rob can have any two things he wants, and Katie, you don't get anything."

Rob was momentarily placated. Katie felt smug with her two toys, and my mailbox remained mysteriously empty.

The next time we were in the vicinity of a Dollar Store, I stopped as I'd promised the kids. "Okay," I reminded them. "This time Rob gets to pick out any two things he wants, and Katie gets zero things."

Rob practically skipped through the door. I handed the money to Katie and found my spot on the bench. About a half hour later, Katie burst through the door, all excited, and skipped right up to me. "Where's your brother?" I asked.

"He's coming."

The door jangled again. There was Rob, dragging his feet, his face etched into a pout. He saw me on the bench and burst into tears again. "Katie made me buy these," he said, holding up the cheap plastic items.

Katie looked up at me, all innocence. "I was just helping him," she said. "You told me to look after him."

"I didn't want her help," Rob said. "I wanted to buy my own stuff."

"Okay, that's it," I said. I took both kids' hands and marched them back into the store. "This time Rob gets to pick out whatever he wants, and Katie, you're going to stand right by me the whole time."

Katie obediently stood next to me, while Rob made his selection. He came back holding a fly swatter.

"You want a fly swatter?" I asked.

"See, I told you it was stupid," Katie said.

"It is not," Rob said.

"Alright, is that what you really want?" I asked.

Rob nodded.

"Well, let's check out."

I handed the dollar bill to the cashier, and we left the store.

There were no tears on the ride home. Rob clutched his fly swatter in the back seat like a trophy from a hard-won battle. Katie sat in the front seat, radiating disdain.

When we got home, Rob immediately ran outside to smack the nearest bush, declaring war on every imaginary insect. Katie turned to me, her face a picture of exasperation.

"You know he's just going to break it in five minutes, right?"

"That's fine," I said. "At least he picked it out himself."

She raised an eyebrow at me, clearly unimpressed. "If you'd just let me handle it, we could've gotten something good."

RESUMÉ ROULETTE

Getting a new airline off the ground is exactly as fun as it sounds. Think spreadsheets, stress, and the ever-present threat of a Federal Aviation Administration officer appearing behind you like a tax auditor with a clipboard.

The FAA could not be more involved, and they aren't there to crack jokes or tell layover stories. Whether it's safety regulations, certifications, funding and grants, or environmental impacts, the FAA is there to breathe down necks, raise blood pressure, and cause the stress-related health problems which then make pilots ineligible to fly.

But it's an important job. Essential. No one would be interested in giving money to an airline run simply by common sense rather than governmental regulations. See? That was a joke. An FAA officer wouldn't get it.

I'd been selected by Vision Airlines to be part of their initial cadre—the core group of captains who'd help launch the airline and train future crews. The days were long, the stress was wide, the workloads certainly over max weight. But we were getting close to the point where we could actually start flying airplanes.

We sat in one of those big meetings, and the FAA appointed check airmen and approved initial cadre captains. I was to be among them. "The next step," the FAA officer said, "is to collect resumés from each of the cadre captains."

I looked around to see each of the other captains pulling out folders with carefully printed resumés inside. When the FAA officer stopped in front of me, I pretended to look around in my bag. "Dang it. I left that folder in my car. I'll need to run out and get it."

He continued collecting resumés and I made a beeline to a telephone.

My daughter, Katie, who was working towards her doctorate in Neuropsychology, answered on the third or fourth ring. "This better be important," she said. "I'm in the middle of rounds."

"Remember when you made me a resumé awhile back?"

She sighed. "Yes."

"Can you send it to me?"

"Dammit Dad, I'm in the middle of residency. Do you even know how busy I am?"

"Katie, I don't ask you for very much, and it would take me all day to sit down and try to figure out how to make a resumé. Can you just take two seconds and fax it over?"

Another sigh. "Fine."

I gave her the fax number, and to my relief, it came

through just as I entered the office. I snatched it out of the machine and headed down the hall. By this time, the meeting with the pilots had broken up, and now the executives were having their turn with the Feds. I knocked on the door and handed over my resumé to the owner of Vision Airlines. He thanked me and I left, closing the door behind me.

I had just enough time to wonder if they were impressed before the first explosion of laughter hit. Then another. And another. At some point, I started to wonder if my resumé was being performed as a stand-up routine.

I called Katie back.

"What now?"

"Why are they all laughing?"

"Who is laughing?"

"I gave them my resumé, and everyone in the room is laughing."

There was a pause. "Let me guess, you didn't even read it, you just handed it to them?"

"Correct."

"You are such a lazy ass when it comes to paperwork. Why didn't you read it?"

In the section of the resumé where it said 'objective,' Katie had typed: "Only interested in a job that's not a pain in my ass. It has to be fun. High pay, low work."

I took a deep breath, listening to the laughter echo down the hall.

"Katie," I said, "I'm either about to get fired or promoted."

She snorted. "Either way, sounds like you got exactly

what you wanted."

Turned out, I did.

I stayed on as one of the founding captains, and we got that airline off the ground—clipboard-wielding FAA and all.

CHIMNEY SWEEP

I was screwing in the last light on the rehab project when the phone rang. The real estate agent had a property she wanted to show us out on Fox Farm Road.

Beth and I had dreamed of this call. We longed for a place in the country with some acreage, with room for our children to grow. As in all real estate decisions, location was a key deciding point. Ideally, the house would still be close enough to town so things like groceries, school, and restaurants remained within easy grasp. And in a perfect world, the house would be close to Eppley Airfield, making my commute bearable. The overwhelming task loomed like retrieving a single luggage bag from a loaded cargo hold. Everything was either too expensive or too far away.

We'd waited so long for this call, we figured we might as well make our current place as comfortable as possible. We did a major rehab on our Brown Street house. The project, mostly cosmetic, left the place looking better than ever. We could see ourselves there for the foreseeable future, which eliminated any need to panic-buy.

But the phone call came the second the project ended.

Our early years of marriage were marked with moving boxes.

We became experts at packing tape, bubble wrap, furniture pads, and heavy lifting. Though we added pets, kids, and rooms along the way, we could estimate within a few cubic feet what size moving truck we'd need. We were good at moving, but that didn't mean we liked it.

We drove out to meet the agent with measured hope. Location-wise, the house on Fox Farm Road checked the box. As we rounded the dirt road, Beth drew in a breath. "I don't even care what the house looks like," Beth said. "Let's buy it."

The property was beautiful, expansive acreage, a barn, and lush plants everywhere.

The house was more of a tearer-downer than a fixer-upper. I thought we should bulldoze it immediately and start from scratch. Beth, buoyed by our recent rehab experience, wanted to make it habitable with the idea we could live there while we built the house we actually wanted.

She won the argument. Though even as I agreed, it felt like Robot from *Lost in Space* shouting in my mind: "DANGER! DANGER!"

Once we moved in, it became obvious the house needed far more than a simple face lift. It needed complete reconstructive surgery. Six years later, of living in a construction zone, we found ourselves in a new conundrum. Now the house was too good to knock down, but just barely. We'd reached the point of no return. We'd bought $30,000 worth of Band-Aids to fix a severed limb. The bleeding wouldn't stop. Talk of building a new house evaporated. The old house would stand.

The termites inhabiting the walls breathed a sigh of relief.

We'd dug our hole, so to speak, and had every intention of filling it with cement, drywall, and stubborn optimism. Each patched wall testified our unwillingness to admit defeat.

But the kitchen barely passed inspection.

The ceilings, less than eight-foot high, hung oppressively over our heads. An old wood-burning stove littered the corner. Though its pipe still snaked up the wall, it existed only for show. According to the guy who sold us the place, the chimney had been removed. For some reason, he'd left behind the stove, though its only purpose as far as I could tell was to take up floor space. No matter the season, the kitchen remained dank and dark. The only window in the room looked out to the garage. A perfect view for someone who liked to gaze at old oil cans, a haphazard mess of tools, and the lawn mower while making a cup of coffee.

Beth had other ideas. "Wouldn't it be great if we could have a vaulted ceiling in here? And what if we turned that window into a door, so we could carry our groceries in from the car? I'm also thinking skylights."

"Not just anybody could build a vaulted ceiling and turn a window into a door," I said, which meant I'd take on the challenge.

The day I began working in the kitchen, my son Rob and I were home alone together. At five years old, he could still be convinced that watching Daddy climb a step stool and poke holes in the ceiling was great fun. I started taking apart the ceiling when I noticed a strange four-by-eight-foot section of drywall. This stood out from the old plaster on the rest of the ceiling. "Strange," I said, giving the drywall a wiggle.

Then I heard a rumble.

"What was that?" Rob asked.

"Not sure, probably just a raccoon that fell down into the wall or something."

Rob's eyes lit up. Our property teemed with nocturnal bandits. Rob, whose love of animals knew no boundaries, had once lured a raccoon into our house with food. The beast wreaked havoc, knocking things from shelves, scratching the walls in a desperate attempt to escape.

The rumble sounded again. Could be a family of squir-rels. Though this sounded heavier. Definitely raccoons, likely a whole gaze of them by the sound of it. Was Rob up to date with his rabies shots? He excitedly edged closer.

I pried back the drywall away from the stud, hoping to catch a glimpse of what we were up against.

But I was not prepared. The gates of hell opened and Satan cried out, "Fire at will!" and God was nowhere to be found. Bricks began tumbling out of the hole and Rob stood right there. With a superhuman burst of speed, I leapt off the stool, tackled Rob into my arms, and flung him into the dining room. Together we crouched and watched as five tons of brick, soot, and rock tormented its way into our kitchen.

I'd removed the ceiling alright.

The chimney, which the previous owner swore he'd removed, along with about a hundred years of ash, collapsed onto the floor.

We stood there open-mouthed and soot-faced. The whites of Rob's eyes were the only color left on his body. No doubt I looked the same.

"Holy crap!" Rob said. "That was awesome! Do it again!"

Immobilized and ankle deep in ash, I couldn't tell how badly the house was destroyed. For all I knew, the outside walls collapsed along with the ceiling.

The front door opened.

"Donald?" Beth walked in and stopped abruptly. She said a thousand things without opening her mouth. And then she did open her mouth.

Rob hadn't started kindergarten yet, but he learned some early lessons on playground language that day. I groped for the ceiling fan in the dining room, thinking I could clear out some of the dust. But the breeze swirled the dust into a tornado.

Beth turned around and walked out.

I couldn't help but be a little offended. I'd just unearthed a ticking time bomb that could have killed any one of us at any moment and furthermore, I'd just heroically saved our son's life.

But I suppose it's hard to see beyond five tons of rubbish in your kitchen. On the bright side, there were no raccoons.

It took three days loading soot and dirt into the front-end loader of our Case 530 tractor. Each bucket weighed around five-hundred pounds and I lost track of how many loads I hauled out. It took several weeks of working every spare moment I had, and even a few I didn't have. We didn't have extra money for eating out. We needed our kitchen.

Since I'd removed the chimney, we now had plenty of room to stretch the ceiling to match the sloped roof. The once-suffocating canopy now uplifted fifteen feet at the highest peak. Near the top, I installed two triangle-shaped windows which cheered the space all day with bright sunlight. The wood-burning stove went into a junk yard somewhere. The window became a door, and now we could access the garage without walking around the house.

No doubt we had our work cut out for us in a continued cycle of mishaps and endless repairs. But when the dust finally settled, we had something more than a functional kitchen. We had memories. Like the house itself, the memories were messy and chaotic, but they were irreplaceable and they were ours.

MISUNDERSTOOD AUTHORITY

"Describe a time when you were in a place of authority and your instructions or desires were misunderstood."

I sat across from the head recruitment officer for American Trans Air. He looked like he'd rather be back in coach next to a crying baby than across the desk from me. Mid-afternoon sun yawned through the window. He'd probably interviewed fifteen pilots before me.

The rolodex of answers flipped through my mind until the perfect story came into focus, and I leaned forward in my chair.

"So there we were, my friend, Bruce Clark and I were flying for ConAgra, and we had a trip out to Scottsdale, Arizona. I don't know if you've spent time in Scottsdale, but there's a lot of money out there."

"You aren't kidding," he said. "The real estate prices are insane."

"Yep. Fancy, impressive hotels and incredible golf

resorts, enough to make your wallet weep, but some people are into that kind of thing."

He shrugged noncommittally.

"We knew there'd be downtime on this trip, and ConAgra booked us in this place called the Cottonwood Resort—great place for kids. Bruce brought along his daughter, Nina, and I brought my son, Rob. The kids were around four or five years old at the time."

The recruitment officer chuckled. "When you travel with kids, it's a trip, not a vacation."

"That's the truth. And we had the whole combo, work and kids. If you ever do make it down to Scottsdale, you should check out the Cottonwood Resort. We stayed in these little bungalows, each with its own swimming pool. The whole place is lined with palm trees, more cactus varieties than I knew existed, red stucco arches, the rugged mountains of the Sonoran Desert contrasting against the ever-blue Arizona sky. It's a beautiful site. It's also hot as hell."

"I'll bet."

"Even though we each had our own little pool, Rob wanted to see the big pool, down in the center of the complex. We had nothing better to do, so we said, 'Sure, let's go check it out.' Middle of summer and it had to be 110 degrees. This type of heat slams you on top of your head, and then the cement kicks it right back at you, so you feel like you're cooking from both directions, top to bottom."

"No thanks. I'd rather be cold than hot."

"For sure," I said. "When we reached the pool, Rob

wasted no time jumping in. He's always been a fish, started swimming at the age of two."

"Good. Teach 'em young."

I nodded. "Bruce, Nina, and I found shade under a bright blue umbrella and we watched Rob and the other hotel guests splash around in the water. After some time, Rob popped out of the water and announced he had to go potty. He knew better than to pee in the pool."

"Smart kid."

"Most definitely. I walked him over to the nearest pool bathroom, but it was under construction. I contemplated the long walk back to our bungalow, rubbed the sweat streaking down the side of my face, and presented my idea to Rob. 'Okay buddy, you know how you aren't supposed to pee in the pool?' Rob nodded vigorously. Pee pee in the pool was a big no no. 'Well, this one and only time, I want you to pee in the pool,' I told him."

The recruiter inched forward, drawn in by the story. "You didn't."

"I did. I said, 'It's too hot to walk all the way back to our rooms. We'll burn the bottoms of our feet. This one time only. Do you understand?' Again, his blond head earnestly bobbed up and down. I patted him on the back and rejoined Bruce and Nina under the umbrella."

"Oh man. I think I know where this is going," the recruiter said.

"Suddenly, Bruce is pounding on my shoulder. 'Ozzy, look!' I followed his gaze, and there Rob stood on the side of the pool, swimsuit down around his ankles, peeing directly into the swimming pool. Before I could formulate words, he shook it off, and jumped right back in."

The head recruiter started with a low chuckle, which escalated into a gasping laugh. He couldn't get his words out. "How'd you handle it?" he managed between guffaws.

"I didn't do a damned thing," I said. "I stayed under that umbrella and watched him swim."

"You let him keep swimming?"

I shrugged. "I figured the damage was done, and there wasn't a checklist procedure for this scenario."

The recruiter wheezed, actually wheezed, slapping the desk. "You're serious?"

"In hindsight, maybe I should've at least looked embarrassed. But honestly? I was too impressed by his confidence."

"I get so damned tired of hearing all these stories about how the pilot was the hero and saved the day," he said, wiping away a tear. "Hell, I don't even care about your credentials and flight hours. You're hired because you're the first pilot today who didn't bore the piss out of me."

"Well, in my experience, sometimes you just have to go with the flow."

BARN BUSTER

I may not be able to juggle flaming swords or solve a Rubik's cube in under ten seconds, but I do have a couple of rare skills which set me apart from the rest of the human population. First, I can fly an airplane. I crunched numbers on this. Of the approximately 8 billion people in the world, only 1.5 million of them have pilot licenses. This sounds like a lot until you start doing the math. If you work out all the calculations, this means 99.98-percent of people in the world cannot fly an airplane. Don't worry. I used a calculator. And Google.

Now, let's talk tractors. Specifically, a Case 530. If you thought pilot stats were exclusive, just wait. I Googled some numbers, did some dubious math, and landed on this: basically nobody on Earth knows how to start a Case 530 except me.

What percentage of the world can both pilot an airplane and operate a Case 530 tractor? I'm guessing it's less than one-percent. Again, I don't claim these are supernatural gifts. Anyone can learn how to do these things, but most people don't.

When my son Rob was around six or seven years old, he'd climb aboard our tan and orange tractor and ride along as I did chores. Starting a Case 530 is about as intuitive as launching a space shuttle using Morse code. First, you had to stick the key in the ignition and turn it enough to warm up the glow plugs—but not too much, or you'd anger the mechanical gods. Jump the gun and the engine could misfire, drain the battery, or refuse to cooperate out of spite. Once the glow plugs were warm, you had to shove the gear shift way over to 'S' to engage the starter, then turn the key further until the engine started to fire.

Meanwhile, you had to finesse the throttle control—located where a modern car's turn signal would be—to inject fuel gradually. Too much, and you'd flood the engine. Too little, and you'd be sitting there with a dead tractor and wounded pride. If all went well, the engine would finally roar to life and you could release the key, letting it settle into the 'on' position.

I never worried anyone would steal the tractor. I was even less worried someone would land a plane on my property and then steal my tractor. But if they did, I wouldn't even press charges. I'd bow down in respect.

When I wasn't on the tractor, I flew planes. And when I wasn't doing either, I usually watched *Family Guy* reruns in random hotel rooms. One day I sprawled out on a hotel bed, flipping through channels when the phone rang.

"Yep," I answered.

"Why the HELL would you teach a small boy how to start a tractor?" My wife, Beth, greeted.

"I didn't."

"Well, Rob just drove the thing through the side of the barn. He got it started, got the front end loader up, and rammed it right through the building."

I wasn't even mad. I was too damned in awe he'd figured out the whole starting sequence, got the front-end loader up, and took out our barn. The feat was impressive—even more so for a little kid.

As years went by, Rob became even more adept at handling the old tractor. He learned all its quirks and became an entrepreneur in our little firewood business. Then, about ten years later, I got another call in a different hotel room.

"The good news is Rob is okay, he doesn't have a scratch on him," Beth said.

"And the bad news?"

"Your tractor is sitting down at the bottom of the hill in three parts."

By this time, Rob was fully initiated into the less than three-percent of the population who could run a Case 530. We'd been using it for years to pull firewood out of the trees when they fell down on our acreage. We'd attach chains to the tractor and drag trees off the big hill straight east of our house. I told Rob a hundred times, "If you are going to get off the tractor when it's running, you've got to push the front end loader down into the ground."

Rob knew that as well as anybody, but one day he got

lazy. The chain slipped off the tree, so he hopped off without bothering to lower the front end. The tractor started rolling. Rob started running. Like a cartoon, the tractor picked up speed. Faster and faster it rolled down the hill, Rob running like Wile E. Coyote after the Roadrunner. The tractor hit an embankment. Time slowed for the briefest moment while the 4,000-pound machine went airborne and came crashing down to the ground. A chunk of the machine fell off the middle and the two front wheels came off entirely. But, it stopped.

I will be forever grateful Rob never caught the tractor. Had he reached the tractor seat and climbed on board, there would have been nothing he could have done to stop the machine and he would have become part of the infinitesimally tiny percentage of the population who have flown a Case 530 tractor. But I'm not sure he'd have lived to tell about it.

After a lot of hard work and some salvaged parts from the junkyard, we actually succeeded in getting it up and running again. Of course, it never ran quite the same, and the steering system was faulty. As we tightened screws, and hammered parts into place, Rob said, "I would've thought you'd be angrier about this. Did you do a lot of stupid stuff when you were my age?"

I wiped my hands on a rag and smirked. "Rob, wrecking a tractor into three pieces doesn't even make the list."

BUSINESS-MINDED

By age 10, my son Rob had already established himself as a doer. For years he ran a successful bunny breeding business. The phrase, "breed like rabbits," guaranteed plenty of new product throughout the year. The bunnies were willing and the profits decent. It took Rob a few years to figure out why his best customer kept returning for more rabbits.

"How many pet bunnies does a person need?" he asked.

Rob's innocence and his business dwindled when he discovered the customer was a butcher selling the meat to a local German restaurant.

I wasn't surprised. The guy struck me as the type who might like to butcher bunnies.

Rob learned the ropes of entrepreneurship by watching my tree business grow. The tree company supplemented my income when the airlines employed me, and took over as my primary income when the airlines laid me off. Either way, I was in the sky—in a bucket truck with a chainsaw, or in a cockpit in the clouds.

Now that he'd reached double digits, Rob figured it was time to start his own business. Starting a business usually requires one of two things: skilled labor or plenty of raw material. Still in elementary school, Rob didn't have years of experience. So, he looked around the farm for inspiration. There were ducks, chickens, and the occasional peacock, but he'd already determined animal husbandry wasn't for him.

But there was no shortage of wood.

Most customers don't want the tree once you cut it down. Part of the service of a tree business is to haul away the mess—the logs, the branches, the old stumps. All that wood came to the farm. Since our house was heated with wood, Rob could already wield an ax. I chunked the big heavy logs on the wood splitter, cut them into four pieces, and then Rob chopped and stacked them.

We had a good system and enough wood to heat our house for a hundred years. And more wood kept coming in.

That's when it dawned on him. Why not sell firewood?

Rob landed on his business venture. I encouraged him to think about his product. What would make his firewood standout from the competition? Customers usually appreciate quality, convenience, and value for their money. Getting the firewood ready would take time. This wasn't like breeding rabbits.

We decided to sell cords of seasoned wood. A cord is about four-by-eight feet and made up of logs about fourteen to sixteen inches. Each cord would consist mainly of hardwood, for cleaner burning, and a touch of maple, to help it easily ignite. Simple enough.

The thing is, you can't burn freshly cut wood, or at least not efficiently. For one thing, it can contain up to fifty-percent moisture. Wet wood creates a lot of smoke, is heavy, and rots easily. Rob's firewood would have to be seasoned. Seasoning firewood is a fancy way of saying it's been stacked properly and dried out. Seasoning the wood required a more precise process.

Once the wood was cut to-size, we stacked it in a crisscross pattern. The spaces between the wood needed to be big enough a mouse could squeeze through, but not so big a cat could chase after it. The spaces allowed for airflow, allowing the wood to dry thoroughly.

Rob had his first lesson in patience. A bunny can pop out a dozen kits in as little as twenty-eight days. Seasoned wood has to dry for a year.

But Rob was a hard worker, determined from a young age.

As his father, I found the process much more difficult.

The waiting part was easy. I've spent half my career waiting in airplane terminals, waiting for the call from the boss, waiting for the weather to clear for takeoff.

The hard part was watching Rob learn the ropes. The first time I handed a chainsaw to a ten-year old kid, all I could do was pray he'd paid attention to the safety instructions. I suppose it's not much different from working as a flight instructor. There's only so much instruction a person can give. Eventually the student must take their first solo flight. Same with using a wood splitter or swinging a maul. Hearing how to do such things isn't the same as doing them. At least flight instruction allows a person to practice with a simulator. There's no such thing for a chainsaw.

As Rob gripped the chainsaw, my heart pounded louder than the engine. Teaching him to stand on his own meant stepping back, even when it felt like letting go of the handlebars on his first bike ride. His skinny arms shook with vibrations. The saw looked deadly in his hands, like a whirling assembly line of savage teeth ready to sever flesh. But he held the saw steady, only flinching a little as it chewed through a knot. When the log broke into two clean pieces, I scanned Rob's fingers, just as I'd done right after his birth, counting to ten, and then counting again. All limbs accounted for, I met his gaze and watched a big smile break out over his face.

Even more painful than handing a ten year-old a chainsaw was watching him learn to back a truck with a trailer attached. It's much easier to do it yourself than watch someone struggle. But that approach doesn't pass on knowledge. Rob wasn't the only one who learned lessons in his business venture. I became an expert in biting my tongue.

After a year of labor, growth, and plenty of splinters, Rob put his first ad in the newspaper. The price was set at $75 for a cord of wood, delivery included. The ad read: split, seasoned, and stacked. Soon, the first order came in. Nothing fuels an entrepreneurial heart like the promise of payment. Rob loaded up the back of the pickup, and I drove him to his first delivery. When we arrived at the property,

Rob eagerly jumped out of the cab and began loading his wheelbarrow. Together, we stacked the wood at the customer's house, our clothes smelling of sweat and oak.

The job finished, Rob stood shyly by the pickup, waiting for me.

"I need you to go up to the door now and collect the money," I told him.

He shook his head. "Can't you do it?"

"Nope."

Still, he didn't budge.

"You want the money, don't you?"

His chin dropped, and his shoulders shrugged.

"In that case, we might as well get in the truck and drive away."

I started to open the door.

"Fine."

He shuffled up to the porch, pressed the doorbell, and waited, looking like a criminal who'd just been given a prison sentence. I hadn't given him any instructions, other than to collect the money.

The customer answered the door. "You done?" he said, looking at the neatly stacked firewood.

Rob stared at his shoes.

The guy handed him a check. Rob accepted the payment, and then turned around and sprinted to the truck as though he'd just burglarized the man. He slipped into the passenger side and stared out the window.

I turned the ignition. "Next time," I said, "you're going to stand there, look them in the eye, and say, 'That'll be $75 and can I put you on our list for next year?'"

Rob's eyes were big.

"There's more to owning a business than delivering the product."

He was quiet on the way to the next delivery. We stacked the wood and he worked as hard as always. Then, unbidden, he approached the door. After a momentary pause he bolstered his courage. He raised his fist and knocked.

Minutes later he came running back to the truck, not to hide, but with a huge smile on his face. "It worked. And he said he'll hire us again next year!"

That first year of business taught Rob a lot. He grew blisters on his hands and dollar signs in his eyes. He conducted himself professionally, mastered eye-contact, and fattened his savings account.

The next year came as a bit of a shock.

"Alright, from now on, you're going to have to pay to use the truck and trailer and you'll need to help pay for the diesel fuel," I told him.

"What? Why?"

"Well, because owning a business isn't only about earning money. It's about paying for expenses."

At the end of the year, he'd increased his work and customer base, but he saw a decrease in his earnings. "I didn't make near as much money as I did last year," he said.

I nodded sympathetically. "Profits come after expenses."

What Rob lost in income that year, he gained in a new

understanding for the value of money. I don't think he ever looked at a twenty-dollar bill again without calculating the amount of work that went into earning it.

Though it was Rob's firewood business, he wasn't legally old enough to drive, so it was a joint venture by necessity. We spent hundreds of hours together, chopping, stacking, and delivering. I'd set out to teach Rob about the pride of ownership, responsibility, and professional development, but the bonding and friendship we developed was the true profit of our hard work.

Firewood was the catalyst for Rob's many successful ventures. Eventually, he used the earnings from the firewood business to invest in a zero-turn mower, which enabled him to start a yard care company. By then he was old enough to hook up the trailer and drive himself to the job sites.

Watching the taillights fade down the driveway, I couldn't decide whether I felt sadness that I wasn't needed for his new business venture, or admiration. I chalked up the pesky lump in my throat to pride. Parenting is all about working yourself out of a job. If Rob didn't need me anymore, I'd done something right. The yard business kept Rob rolling in cash throughout his high school years. He'd amassed a large customer base and his business was well-enough established that he was able to sell it.

Throughout his adult years, Rob has never been without a side- hustle. The only difference is now I go to him for advice. And when he discovers a promising new business venture, I join in, but I usually let him do the driving.

SOAKED AND SNAKED AT SIXTH AND MAIN

New Orleans has Mardi Gras. Holland, Michigan, celebrates Tulip Time. And Gilroy, California, takes pride in its Garlic Festival. Chadron, Nebraska, hosts its own unique celebration: Fur Trade Days.

Celebrated since 1977, Fur Trade Days honors the area's rich history as a significant site for fur trading in the early 19th century. Chadron finally earned its place on the map in 1885 when it became a stop on the Fremont, Elkhorn, and Missouri Valley Railroad. The name 'Chadron' derived from French fur trader Louis Chartran, who trapped and traded in the region.

Trading beaver pelts may have lost its appeal over the past two centuries, yet those with deep roots in western Nebraska feel the draw to return home every second weekend in July. This is the weekend of high school class reunions, beer gardens, street parties, softball tournaments, 5-10K races, open-air markets, barbecues, live music on the court-house lawn, and the World Championship Buffalo Chip Competition, in which people literally chuck dried buffalo poop down Main Street. Fur Trade Days brings the excitement of the carnival, which complicates parking and inconveniences local businesses, but delights young children. The weekend boasts an authentic buckskinner's camp for the historically minded, a time travel journey to the area's beginnings.

I like going downtown, catching up with old friends, taking in the live bands—especially if Crazie Louie's playing. After all, they've been rocking Nebraska since the '60s and even landed a spot in the Nebraska Music Hall of Fame.

But the weekend's most well-attended feature is the annual Fur Trade Days Parade.

Just mention the parade and I can smell truck exhaust, the sulfuric-rotten-egg scent of gunshot residue from the fur trade reenactors, and fresh horse manure slapping against burning hot pavement. I can hear the ear-piercing shrill of proud firetrucks, the sputters of the Shriner's mini-cars racing in circles, and the clatter of candy thrown at the feet of eager children.

As in real estate, location is everything in parade watching. Those with property on Main Street can sit on their front porches with coffee in-hand, or dust off the lawn chairs from their storage sheds and watch from the comfort of their yards. For the rest of us, we have to grab curb spaces wherever we can squeeze our butts, huff chairs, water bottles, and crying children. Parade-route seating is an unofficial competition of the weekend.

But if you can't live on Main Street, the second-best option is to have a friend who does.

For many years, my childhood best friend, Kenny Groves, lived in one of the most sought-after parade-watching spots in town. The Spanish-style stucco house sat atop a sloped lawn, which boasted an enviable amount of shade from the Chinese Elm trees bordering the property. Located at Sixth and Main Street, you could hardly hope for a better spot. Of course, those who own houses directly across from the courthouse would probably claim the better view, but we'd never have gotten away with our shenanigans had Kenny lived anywhere else.

The float entries are anything from advertisements for local businesses, area pageant winners, local and state politicians, and class reunions, to the ever-present Shriner cars, emergency vehicles, and 4-H Clubs. Some parade floats get creative with their design skills, but the vast majority hook a trailer to a pickup, fill a tank with water, and arm themselves with Super Soakers. Another unofficial competition of the weekend begins as soon as the Color Guard walks by and everyone stands to salute the red, white, and blue. Once Old Glory has passed, it's fair game for float riders to start aiming water guns at unsuspecting parade goers. A person can never know for sure whether they'll receive candy or a blast of cold water. In Nebraska in mid-July the temperatures can creep past 100 degrees, so usually no one gets too bent out of shape about the quick cool down.

Usually.

We all gathered on Kenny's front lawn, waiting for the parade to start. That year was a highlight for me because I made the drive to Chadron with my son, Rob. We were surrounded by my friends—Kenny, Keith Reid, Dan Wild, Fred Schlickbernd—a whole bunch of guys firmly in their fifties who were old enough to know better, but young enough to still do things simply for the shits and giggles.

Kenny had a history of practical jokes. He had the largest collection of prank toys—fake dirty diapers, critters jumping out of cans, whoopee cushions, electric shocking gum, and more rubber snakes than ought to be legal to own. And as owner and operator of the town's successful business, Tree Doc, Kenny had access to even bigger toys. Instead of sitting on the lawn dodging little squirts of water, we'd be ready with a little defensive plan of our own.

We used Kenny's bucket truck to hoist water sprinklers into the giant elm trees which formed a canopy over Main Street. The branches and sprinklers arched elegantly, reaching down at just the right angle to welcome each float as it passed underneath. We ran hoses from the sprinklers to the spigot next to Kenny's house.

The crowds lining the route further south on Main started to stand, signaling the Color Guard had likely arrived at Seventh Street. One more block and they'd be at Sixth and Main.

We stood, removed our hats, and giggled like middle school boys who'd just seen their first naked girl in a magazine. As the flag marched proudly by, we tried to think somber thoughts to keep from bubbling over in laughter. We placed our hands over our hearts and pledged that this parade would go down in Fur Trade history.

Being the gentlemen we were, we didn't hose Miss Chadron or Miss Northwest, and as long as the parade floats were just throwing candy, we let them pass in peace. But as soon as someone would pull out a squirt gun, Kenny nodded at his son, Logan, who was manning the spigot, to turn the hoses on full blast.

A thousand bats at nighttime couldn't have matched the screeching heard up and down Main Street each time a new float fell victim. The float riders would just be filling up their water guns, ready to blast us, when out of nowhere buckets of water dumped out of a cloudless sky. As an extra treat, Kenny's wife was riding in the parade. Unbeknownst to the rest of us, Kenny had slipped the float driver a $20 bill before the start of the parade. When it rolled up in front of the house, it didn't just slow down, but came to a complete halt.

I can remember sitting there, watching Kenny's wife mouthing cuss words at Kenny, but her sounds disappeared in a strange gurgle as her mouth filled with water. By the time the sodden float moved forward again, water trailed behind it, dripping all the way down Main Street.

To add to all this, Kenny brought out one of his big rubber snakes, a particularly realistic model—black, coiled, and pliable. He affixed the snake to the end of a fishing wire, and put my son, Rob, in charge of the fishing pole. Whenever anyone stepped close to the snake, Rob gave the line a little tug, and the snake reared up out of its coiled position and scared the bejesus out of the closest victim.

There we were, grown men who should have known better, just laughing our asses off. I kept yelling, "Rob, you'd better stop doing that. You are going to give someone a heart attack!" But then he'd do it again, and we were lost in another cycle of laughing so hard it felt like our stomachs might come out our noses. Rob and Logan had the perfect comedic timing. The parade walkers were so focused on the water coming down from the trees, they didn't pay attention to the ground. Then the snake's movement caught their attention, and you'd have thought the town opened an insane asylum right in front of Kenny's house.

Throughout the hour-long parade, people were constantly getting drenched then startled by the snake. You'd hear screams and see people running away in surprise. The parade route starts just before Tenth Street and ends down by the railroad tracks, so as the first float riders finished, they looped back to Kenny's house to witness the trickery they'd fallen for. They also wanted to watch others get soaked and snaked. The Germans have a word for this— 'schadenfreude,' the pleasure of witnessing the misfortune or discomfort of others.

Kenny's lawn was packed with onlookers eager to witness the prank in action. This big ol' cowboy strode down the street in his Justin boots and belt buckle he'd likely won from wrestling a bull to the ground with one hand tied behind his back. He had one of those wide-brimmed hats and an even wider frame. If a person had to bet against this guy or the wildest bucking bronco in the west, you'd slam your money down on the cowboy's side of the table. We started making unofficial bets as soon as we saw him. There was no way he'd be scared of a rubber snake. You expect kids, ladies, and people like me to be scared of a snake, but this guy would likely stomp the thing into the ground with his heel, or take out his knife and separate its rubber head from its slithery body.

Just as he came into position, Rob tugged the line and the snake rose from the cement with just the right amount of realism.

That's when it happened.

The cowboy let out the loudest, highest pitch scream, so loud it shattered any illusions of his rugged image.

A chorus of laughter erupted as he bolted down Main Street, his boots clapping against the pavement like a panicked stampede. All the people my age nearly wet our pants, even though we hoped we hadn't sent anyone to an early grave. We were still laughing when the last police car drove past, signaling the end of the parade. Kenny invited everyone in for donuts and coffee, and his house was full. Everyone on that block had a stomachache from laughing so loud and so long. Laughter filled the air as friends recounted the chaos; and the camaraderie reminded me why Fur Trade Days is such a cherished tradition.

I'm still surprised we didn't kill anyone with a heart attack that day, but come to think of it, I never did see that cowboy again.

DEAD HEAT

I slipped my hotel key into the pocket of my gym shorts and took the elevator to the ground floor. When they named the NBA team *Miami Heat*, I imagine they were trying to evoke the reality native Floridians endure with a daily acceptance: the heat in this town can and will crush you. For this reason, I headed out the door before the sun fully had a chance to rise and wilt my desire for self-improvement.

After some half-hearted stretches, I started jogging. If I exercised now, I could later guiltlessly inhale Cuban sandwiches. I'd flown into Miami the previous afternoon for work and had a few days to kill before I'd be back at the airport for the next leg of my journey.

I didn't like the looks of this neighborhood. Too many gas stations with boarded up windows, too many lots with barbed wire fences. When my boss booked our rooms at a hotel near the airport, I'd complained about its location.

"Don," he'd said. "It's two days. Nothing is going to

happen."

I reasoned this to be true. Most of the city still slept at this early hour anyway. I wouldn't be as apt to run these same paths at night. Miami is a city known for its vibrant nightlife and prefers a slower wake time than where I'd grown up in the Midwest. Clearly this peninsula city preferred a more laid-back approach to life, and I couldn't fault it one bit.

The jogging path meandered through palm-tree-lined streets. My legs felt great and my body loose, the last remaining kinks of sleep slipping away with each step.

I squinted in the distance. Something lay across the path. My first thought? Alligator.

But as I got closer, the shape didn't look right. Discarded trash bags? Made sense in this neighborhood.
I calculated my ability to hurdle over the top of the roadblock. A simple hop at most. As I soared over the debris, my brain registered it a second too late—this wasn't trash. It was a body.

My brain flashed a warning light. I turned back around, walking this time, my eyes on the figure before me. Something about the angle of the body seemed off. I inched closer. "Hey, are you okay?"

No answer.

I inched closer still. "Excuse me, do you need help?" And then I stood over the top of her. The lifeless eyes of a young woman stared back at me. Blood soaked into the sidewalk around her, leaving a dark brown stain. She was beyond help.

I took off at a sprint, but not down the jogging path. I cut through flower beds and over a small bush. A gas station sat near the other side of the park. If I'd had a stopwatch, I may have been able to set a new world record in the 200-meter dash.

The man behind the counter seemed reluctant to hand over the corded phone even after the words "dead body" came out of my mouth.

Perhaps the Miami lifestyle was a bit too laid back.

The phone finally in-hand, I dialed 9-1-1.

"Stay right there," the operator said. "Someone will be there soon."

I waited outside the gas station, avoiding the glare of the attendant, who seemed rather peeved I'd used his phone without making a purchase.

The sirens wailed in the distance, and soon the flashing blue police lights interrupted the soft rays of early morning. "Are you Don Osborn?" a thin cop with glasses asked.

"Yes sir."

"Take us to the body."

I led them back to the scene, and watched as three policemen gathered around the woman. One knelt down and held his fingers to the corpse's neck. "No pulse." The other two nodded grimly. Clearly Miami had sent out its finest for this job.

Once the obviously dead woman had been declared deceased, the police turned their attention on me.

"Where are you from?"

"Omaha."

"And what are you doing in Miami?"

"I'm a pilot. I flew in yesterday."

"And how long are you here for?"

"Just a couple of days."

"We're going to need to see some ID."

"I don't have any, just my hotel key." I pulled it out of my pocket.

"Isn't it a bit strange you don't have any identification on you?"

"Not really. I don't usually carry it while jogging."

"What hotel are you staying at?"

"The Sheraton, like it says on my key card."

"And how did you discover the body?"

"Like I said, I was out running. I came across this—" I gestured downwards. "I ran to the gas station and called you guys."

"What was the state of the body when you discovered it?"

"Dead."

The cops exchanged looks. "Listen, you'll need to come with one of us."

"Where to?"

"Back to your hotel room. We need to see your identification."

"Is this really necessary? If it's all the same to you, I'd like to finish my workout and get on with my day."

"You'll be coming with me," the mustached cop said.

By this time, a news crew gathered on the street outside the gas station. The city, disturbed from sleep, arose and filmed yet another death. We walked back to the car, leaving the other two cops to take photographs, jot down notes, and do whatever else police have to do when they find a dead body in the middle of a jogging path.

"Hop in," the cop said. The lights on the car flashed blue and red streaks across my eyes.

I reached for the door handle.

"You can ride in the back," he said.

"Are you serious?"

He looked serious.

I climbed in the back of the car. The cop turned on the siren. It's not easy to make conversation over the sound of a police wail, and I gave up the attempt. My morning routine dashed, I mentally planned out the rest of the day. It would soon be too hot to run outside. I could give the gym treadmill a try. More likely, I'd change into my swimsuit and soak in the hot tub. Was it too early to find Simpsons' reruns on the TV?

The police officer pulled in front of the hotel, and a few people stopped to stare. Guests looked up from their complimentary breakfasts to watch the cop escort me to the front desk. The woman behind the check-in counter stood at attention, looking me up and down as though I'd already been prosecuted for a crime. "How can I help you?"

"I'm looking up a guest registration," the officer said. "Is Don Osborn registered here?"

She clacked away at the keyboard. "Osborn...yes, he checked in yesterday afternoon."

"Room number please?"

"Let's see," clickety clack clack. "Looks like 247."

"Thank you."

"Let me know if there's anything else I can do for you."

"Yes ma'am, I will," he said. Then turning to me. "Okay, to the elevator."

"Seriously? She just confirmed I'm staying here."

Again, he looked serious. We entered the elevator, which made no attempt at speed records. The doors inched shut, the elevator crawled upward, then lurched to an unsteady halt before creaking open again.

I walked in the direction of my room, stopped at the door, and pulled out my key. It opened on the first try, and the policeman followed me into my room, which was littered with the clothes I'd tossed around from the previous day.

"ID please."

I found my wallet on the dresser counter and retracted my Nebraska Driver's License. The officer took it in his hand and read it over. "Alright, this checks out." His demeanor seemed friendlier once he decided I hadn't killed anyone. He placed the license back in my hand and reached into his own pocket for a business card. "If you remember anything else, be sure to give us a call."

"Will do," I said.

*

Later that night, I called my wife at our predetermined time. The TV provided the only light in the room. I'd turned the channel to a local news station, but muted the volume. Beth and I had an agreement. We kept our calls short, because of the high cost of long-distance. We'd each talk for about five minutes, give the highlights of our day, and then hang up.

Beth went first. The kids had a lot going on. Katie tried out for the gymnastics team. Rob's pet duck trailed him everywhere around the farm, a hindrance in trying to get to school in the mornings. Usually these conversations kept me going. I missed my family terribly, but this night, my thoughts were elsewhere.

While Beth told me about a roundoff flip or some other trick Katie mastered back in Nebraska, my eyes focused on the TV screen in front of me. Right there on NBC 6 South Florida, I watched footage as policemen loaded a shirtless man into the back of their police car.

"That's him! I bet that's the guy who killed her!"

"Huh?" Beth said.

"Sorry, I was talking to the TV."

The guy looked guilty as hell, loaded into the backseat, the cop pushing on the top of his head. He should get the death penalty, killing a woman so young. She couldn't have been more than twenty-one. I read the closed captioning on the screen. "Morning jogger finds dead body, suspect questioned." I looked closer at the screen. *Well damn, that's me!* I watched myself being loaded into the back of a cop car.

"Oh Donald," Beth's voice interrupted my thoughts. "I am so sorry. I've gone over my time."

"Huh?" I looked at my watch.

"Do you have anything to report?"

We had about 30 seconds left before this call went over

budget. "Not too much. Found a dead body, called the cops, got questioned by police, and now I'm watching myself get into a cop car on the news. It was 92-degrees here today. The heat in this city is deadly. Alright, gotta go. Tell the kids I love them."

A HOT DOG AND A FUNERAL

I strolled in the enigma of a perfect Chicago day. Normally the winds bounce off Lake Michigan with the strength to bowl a person over, but today there was only a slight breeze. For once the thermometer avoided extremes and allowed the mercury to settle somewhere in the pleasant middle.

It was the perfect day for a funeral.

Chicago's most famous resting place for the dead is Graceland Cemetery, located on the North Side. The cemetery features ornate mausoleums and sculptures, a few of which were designed by Louis Sullivan. Once known as the "Father of Skyscrapers," Mr. Sullivan became a permanent resident of Graceland after his death in 1924. Other famous people buried there include George Pullman, inventor of the Pullman sleeping car, and Marshall Field, a pioneer in the retail industry and the founder of what was once the world's largest department store.

But I wasn't thinking about death as I strolled past the wrought-iron gate entrance. My mind was on less existential matters, namely the Chicago-style hot dog I'd bought off a street vendor the previous evening. I couldn't wait to have another one.

As I contemplated hot dogs and dinner plans, a slow caravan of cars began passing by me. Someone had died. A black hearse led the procession into the famed cemetery followed by at least a hundred vehicles. Due to the unusually nice weather, many passengers rode with their windows down. It would have been polite to turn my head and mind my own business, but funerals and car crashes have a similar effect: it's impossible to look away.

So, I looked. And then looked again. The strangest feeling came over me. Each time a car passed by, I could have sworn I recognized the person inside. My mind felt detached from my body as though I floated above and watched each familiar face go by. All thoughts of hot dogs disappeared, and existential crises moved into full throttle. Had I died? By God, was this my funeral? If it was, should I attend? Would there be Chicago-style hot dogs at the reception?

Resisting the urge to follow the stream of cars into Graceland, I continued back to my hotel room. It seemed to take increased concentration to move one leg in front of the other. The physical effort was akin to running away from a monster in a dream, wanting to go fast, then realizing your legs are underwater.

Who were all those people in the cars? Friends? Distant

family members? Strangers I'd passed in airports? Why did they seem so oddly familiar?

I felt relief as I stepped into my hotel room. Dead people couldn't operate key cards, right? Kicking off my shoes, I collapsed onto the bed, letting exhaustion pin me to the mattress. For a long while, I stared blankly at the white ceiling, my mind grappling with the surreal events of the day. This wasn't déjà vu; to the best of my knowledge, I'd never wandered past a cemetery to my own funeral before. This was something else entirely. Vuja de, perhaps?

At least the funeral had been well attended. The traffic downtown must have been a nightmare with that many cars creeping along at three miles per hour. At least I'd been walking. Imagine being dead and stuck in traffic! Though I suppose at that stage, a person wouldn't be in a hurry to get anywhere. Could dead people be stuck in traffic? Seemed like a good sign I could wonder about these things at all. Dead people can't think. Wouldn't Descartes say that was proof enough I was alive? Forget, "I think, therefore I am.' How about, 'I think, therefore I'm not dead?"

Still feeling out of sorts, I turned on the local news. I needed something to distract me from this bizarre swirl of thoughts. They were reporting on the funeral of Roger Ebert, the famed thumbs-up movie critic. He'd been eulogized at Chicago's Holy Name Cathedral and then buried at Graceland Cemetery down the street from my hotel.

The news reporter was interviewing famous people who attended the service. The TV pulled me forward. I studied their faces. Most of them were famous enough to be recognizable, but not well-known enough to me that I could put a name to any of them. Some of them I'd seen only a few hours ago, driving by in cars.

No wonder the passengers looked so familiar in the funeral procession. These were public figures who'd passed through my life through movies, interviews, and media. This whole weird afternoon became clarified in a two-minute news broadcast.

It was such an uncanny feeling, experiencing something so surreal and yet entirely explainable. At any rate, it was nice to know I wasn't dead. Glancing at the clock, I sat up and pulled on my shoes. I needed to hurry if I was going to get to the hot dog stand before it closed.

EVERYBODY HATES YOU

Life was good.

For a solid year I'd been gainfully employed as a pilot for ConAgra. It wasn't easy keeping a job in the airline industry. A pilot could be hired one day and fired the next with even the smallest fluctuation in the economy. The easiest way for a company to tighten a budget is to sell a few airplanes. Next to go are the pilots.

Not only had I flown with the same company for more than twelve months, I'd already made captain, flown more hours than anyone else, and I genuinely liked my coworkers.

Jim, my boss, seemed to like me and always greeted me with friendly pleasantries. I practically skipped into my annual review, already imagining my raise and bonus check.

"Sit down," Jim said, as I entered his office.

"Thanks." I took the seat across from him.

He flipped through some papers on his desk. "Look, I

don't know what we're going to do," he said. "This isn't easy for me."

It felt as though my chair dropped about ten thousand feet in altitude. "Oh?"

"Listen, you are an excellent pilot."

I nodded.

"I've had excellent feedback from customers. Seems like the passengers really like you."

"Glad to hear it."

"But . . ."

This 'but' felt big enough to require two airplane seats.

"But," he said again. "Everybody hates you."

"Huh?"

"I've had complaints from every pilot in this company. You're hard to work with. No one can stand to be around you."

I opened my mouth, trying to swallow the information. "I . . . I," I stammered. "I know for a fact Bruce Clark didn't say anything bad about me." Bruce was one of my closest friends. We'd been flying together for years.

"You'd be surprised," Jim said. "The good news is I'm not going to fire you. You are too good a pilot. But I can't give you a raise with this type of performance report."

"I understand," I said.

"Well, thanks for coming in, Don."

He stood. I stood. We shook hands. And I walked out of the office chewing on the shit sandwich I'd just been fed.

About a week later I was flying with Kirk Fitcher. I wasn't in the mood to talk. I only uttered words that pertained to the operation of the airplane. We were staying the night in an Embassy Suites. The hotel was built like an oval around the commissary at the bottom. Each floor of rooms opened to balconies which overlooked the continental breakfast, seating areas, and indoor fountains. Our rooms were up on the tenth floor.

I held my key card to the lock.

"Are you going down to dinner?" Kirk asked.

"No. I'm not hungry," I said. "I'm not going to eat."

"What's with you? You've been surly all day."

"I'm fine."

"You are not. You've barely said five words to me."

"Just drop it," I said.

I kicked my roller bag through the door and quickly stepped inside. I went to push the door closed behind me, but Kirk stuck his foot in the door frame.

"Move your foot," I said.

"I'm not going anywhere until you tell me what's wrong."

"Oh, like you don't know."

His face was blank, as though he didn't actually know. "I have no idea what you're talking about."

This succeeded in making me angrier. "I know there's ass kissers in this company, but I didn't think you'd be one of them."

Kirk pushed his hand against my door. "Did you flunk the mental health test?"

I swung open the door and stood chest-to-chest with Kirk. "You either get out of my way or you are going over this ledge."

"Lay off it, Don. I'm coming in this room and we're going to sit down and talk because I need to know what the hell is going on."

I turned on my heel and retreated back into my room. Kirk followed me. The more he spoke, the madder I got. It was evident he was trying to weasel out of this and come up with excuses. But I also knew I wouldn't actually throw him over the ledge at the Embassy Suites.

"Fine." I sat on my bed, not offering Kirk a seat. "I had my review last week." I started explaining my review, how it started out great and quickly took a turn. "I know about how all of you guys hate me, how you don't want to be around me, but you know what? You can kiss my ass. Unlike you guys, I have the resumé to actually get another flying job somewhere else."

Kirk held up his hands. "Whoa. Wait a minute. How long have you been here?"

"Just over twelve months," I said. "It was my annual review."

"Oh my God," he said. "You got the everybody hates you speech."

"The what?"

"The everybody hates you speech," he repeated. "We all got that same speech at our first review. Jim never budgets enough to cover the whole staff, so someone has to take a hit. It's always the new guy."

"What?"

"Yeah. If Jim comes in under budget, he gets a big fat

bonus check. So every year, he's gotta pick out someone to be on the barrel. This year it was you."

"So everybody doesn't hate me?"

"Not everybody."

"Wait, some people hate me?"

"Heck, I don't know. I haven't heard of anyone who hates you, but if you go around threatening to throw all your friends over the balcony, I imagine you aren't the most well-liked guy around."

I shrugged. "Sorry about that."

"You hungry?"

"Starved."

"Let's go grab dinner."

I pocketed my key card and we headed towards the elevator. "Maybe we should draft a letter to Jim from all the pilots saying everybody loves me so much I deserve a raise," I suggested.

Kirk snorted. "Yeah, let me know how that works out."

I laughed, hitting the elevator button. "Miracles happen."

Kirk smirked as the doors slid shut. "An everybody loves Don letter is far too unbelievable."

ERROR 404: FLOPPY DISK MISHAP

The ringing of the hotel phone interrupted my one-man-shower concert. I wrapped a towel around my waist and hurried out of the bathroom. My hair still dripped when I answered the call.

"Yep."

"Hey Don, are you busy?"

"Nope."

"Good, 'cause I can't figure out this computer."

Back in the old days, in the 1900s, people didn't carry personal contact devices with them at all times. When the phone rang, you answered it.

"What seems to be the problem?" I asked.

"I don't know what to do after inserting this operating system CD into the tower."

My wife, Beth, and I had just purchased our first desktop computer, a Gateway 2000. The newest technological wave was coming towards us and we had no intention of being pulled out to sea. I'd seen a few news reports about some far-fetched idea called the World Wide Web. I'd also seen a lot of episodes of Star Trek. As far as I was concerned, the idea of this World Wide Web becoming a reality seemed as likely as Spock cracking a joke. I figured we'd at least see what the fuss was about MS-DOS.

"Gosh," I said, "I don't know any more about this computer stuff than you do. But hey, Kirk is right next door. He's a whiz at this stuff."

Kirk Fitcher and I flew for the same company. We were in a hotel for the night and they'd given us adjoining rooms. I knocked on his door. "Hey, got a minute to talk to Beth about some computer stuff?"

"Sure thing."

I arranged for Beth to call Kirk's number, since my phone cord wouldn't stretch that far. He eyed my towel. I shrugged and followed him into his room, eager to learn whatever Kirk was willing to teach.

As Kirk rattled off his jargon, I felt as though I'd accidentally stumbled into a Starfleet briefing. Was I supposed to take notes, salute, or just nod and hope for the best?

"Did you insert the MS-DOS setup disk into the floppy drive or CD-ROM?"

Disk? Floppy drive? Was Kirk talking dirty to my wife?

"You might need to format the hard drive," he said.

Hard drive? Really Kirk. You can't be serious.

"Don't worry, this might be confusing the first time."

I could only hear half the conversation, but he was right.

I was confused.

"If the floppy disk drive light is stuck on, you may have the disk inserted upside-down. Take it out and try again. Don't pull out the floppy disk too quickly, or you might corrupt the files. You may need to tell the system to unmount before ejecting it."

Unmount? Eject? Good God.

"Whatever you do, don't touch the shiny part on the disk."

Should I pry the phone out of Kirk's hand? Protect my wife's honor?

"Well, if the screen is blank, perhaps the brightness isn't turned on?"

I was pretty sure it was turned on by now.

This went on far longer than it should have. I don't think I learned anything about computers. But I was certainly more eager to get my hands on one soon.

Finally Kirk ended the call. "Glad I could help. You wanna talk to Don? Sure, I'll tell him."

He hung up.

"She said she had to go. I guess we ran up the phone bill."

"I'll say," I muttered.

"What's that?"

"Nothing. I better get back to my room, put some clothes on."

"Please do."

I tugged on the interior door. "Uh oh," I said.

"What do you mean 'uh oh'?"

"My door is locked."

"Yeah, those doors lock automatically. You have to use your key."

We both looked down at the white towel around my waist.

"You don't have a key, do you," he said.

"Where exactly do you think I'd keep it?"

Thankfully, he didn't respond.

"Can I use your phone?" I asked. "I'll call the front desk and have them meet me up here with a key."

Kirk's eyes widened in alarm. "No way."

"Seriously? It'll take just a minute."

I stepped forward, but Kirk blocked my path. "You can't call the front desk," he said. "What will they think?"

"They'll think I locked myself out."

"But you are a naked man in my room. How's that going to look?"

"I don't really care. We're never going to see any of these people again."

Kirk wrung his hands together. "Okay, I have a plan. I'm going to pretend to be you. I'll call the front desk, and you hide in the bathroom."

"The bathroom? Are you serious?"

Kirk's eyes said he was serious.

"Fine."

I would have waved my white towel in defeat, but didn't figure it would improve the situation. Kirk made the call, then shooed me into the bathroom. "Don't make a sound," he said.

A few minutes later I heard the knock on the door. That was my cue. I pushed the bathroom door open. There was the front desk worker handing a key over to Kirk.

"Who is this, Kirky?" I said.

"Oh God," Kirk said.

The front desk worker glanced at me, then quickly looked away. "Have a nice day," he said, his words floating into the hallway as he made a hasty exit.

Kirk followed him. "Wait, let me explain." The front desk man walked faster. Kirk chased after him. "It's not what it looks like."

Fortunately, Kirk dropped my room key on his rush out the door. I picked it up off the floor and unlocked our adjoining room. It would be nice to get out of this wet towel and into some clean clothes.

From that day forward Kirk was no longer just my copilot and go-to tech guy, he was Kirky and he never lived it down.

FOOL ME TWICE

Bruce Clark's trust in people was almost a super-power—but not a useful one. He was a good enough human that if someone told him something, he believed it. He figured the world was a decent place full of people who didn't cuss, lie, or eat junk food. Just like him.

Heaven only knows why he befriended me. Believe me, I gave him plenty of reasons to reconsider during the years we flew together in the cockpit.

Bruce subscribed to a water delivery service. Each week a truck pulled up and left a five-gallon jug on his front porch. One day we were hanging around after a flight, and Bruce said he had to hurry up and get home, because he didn't want his water sitting on the porch all afternoon.

"Bruce," I said. "I can't believe you are paying for that."

"Why not?"

"I was driving past your house the other day, and saw the water guy using your hose to fill up your jug."

"Are you serious?"

"I am."

"Well that just makes me mad."

"It should."

"I'm going to call them right now and give them a piece of my mind."

"I would if I were you."

Most people who knew me wouldn't have fallen for it. But Bruce took it—hook, line, and sinker. I let him get as far as dialing the number before I told him I was kidding.

Despite the ongoing shenanigans, Bruce remained a faithful friend. I never figured out how such an incredibly intelligent guy could be so gullible; but for him trust came from someplace deeper. Of course, a better person wouldn't have taken advantage of Bruce's innocence. But the comedic payoff proved too great to resist.

We took a job flying into a small town in Alabama. We were hungry with no restaurants in sight and certainly nowhere to rent a car. The airport manager, who doubled as the town's mayor, pointed us to the yellow phone on the wall. "There's only one taxi in town, but you can call him up and he'll take you where you need to go."

The taxi service answered on the second ring. Fifteen minutes later an old guy showed up in his personal car. We understood about every third word he said, because his accent was as thick as kudzu. But he seemed to understand us and drove us to the only restaurant in town. "I'll just wait around and take you back to the airport when you're done," he told us.

That suited us fine, because it seemed like a hassle to track him down again. At any rate, we went inside where I had the first fried bologna sandwich of my life. This wasn't the thin sliced bologna you buy in the grocery store. It was thick, fried crisp at the edges, topped with mayonnaise, pickles, lettuce, tomato, American cheese melted over the top, and a splash of hot sauce between two pieces of Wonder Bread.

Stuffed with fried bologna and regret, we climbed back into the taxi. When we reached the airport, the old guy turned around and said, "That'll be $50."

Bruce and I exchanged a look—part shock, part financial despair. Fifty dollars was an unheard of amount of money to pay for a taxi ride back then, but Bruce pulled out two twenties and a ten and handed it over. "Can we get a receipt?" The man scrounged around on the floor of his car, until he came up with a crumpled piece of paper. He made a show of smoothing it out and finding a pen. He scrawled the numbers and handed the paper to Bruce.

We thanked him and walked back inside the FBO.

"How were things?" the airport manager/mayor asked.

"Well, the bologna sandwich was great, but fifty bucks for a cab drive was crazy," I said.

"Fifty dollars?"

"Yeah," I said. "Show him the receipt, Bruce."

Bruce held it out.

"Oh my God," the mayor said. "I'm going to call Leroy and talk to him. If he wants airport business, he's going to have to be more reasonable. That's just ridiculous." He pulled out his wallet, counted $50, and handed it over to Bruce. "I don't want you thinking bad of our little town. Don't you worry. I'll get this settled with Leroy."

Somewhere below, Alabama faded into the distance. In the cockpit, Bruce clung to the receipt like it was evidence in a crime drama.

"No one would know if you turned in that receipt," I told Bruce. "A big company won't miss fifty dollars."

Bruce was honest, but even he struggled to see a real victim in double-dipping on a taxi fare. He kept debating it, still arguing with himself as we landed and called it a night.

The next morning, we had another early flight. Once we were in the air, I asked, "So, what did you decide about the receipt?"

"I'm not proud of myself, but I'm going to turn it in," he said.

"Good for you. That's what I would have done."

This didn't bring him comfort, and I could tell the guilt ate him up inside. "Did you see the news this morning?" I asked.

"What news?"

"That little town we stopped in yesterday?"

"What about it?"

"Apparently some cab driver got fired, and he went home, hooked up a manure spreader to the back of his car, and spread shit all down the main road in some act of retribution."

"Really?"

"Yep. And he wasn't only the taxi driver. He was also

the town dog catcher. He let all the shelter dogs loose. They tore through Main Street, rolled in manure, then stormed City Hall like a four-legged riot. I guess the mayor's office was in pretty bad shape."

"Oh my God! Do you think it's the same guy?"

"Seems like it could be. Didn't the airport manager say there was only one cab driver in town?"

Bruce swallowed. "That's right."

"They say he might get twenty years' jail time for criminal mischief. Luckily his kids will be old enough to get jobs soon, otherwise I'm not sure what they'd do without his income."

"He was pretty old to have young kids."

"Good point. And now he'll be dead before he gets out of jail."

"Where did you hear this?"

"USA Today," I said.

"But we don't carry that one on the airplane."

"Right, this was back at the hotel."

The rest of the flight, Bruce brooded. I could tell he mulled everything over. He looked a little green.

As soon as the wheels touched down, Bruce bolted like his seat was on fire, hunting for a USA Today. Once the passengers unloaded, I found Bruce maniacally tearing through a newspaper. "Surely it couldn't be in the sports pages," he muttered.

He looked up and saw me watching him, a big grin on my face. He dropped the paper and tore after me, tackling me into a La-Z-Boy, toppling it over. "Are you ever going to quit doing that to me?" he yelled.

Of course, I was laughing and several people stopped to stare at us, wondering whether they should call the cops. With a final shove, Bruce climbed off me and stomped over to a chair in the corner.

"Come on Bruce. I'm just trying to help you mature and learn the ways of life."

He forgave me, like he always did, because Bruce was a good man. Unfortunately, they say the good die young, and it was true in Bruce's case. We lost him to a crop dusting accident.

I, on the other hand, might live forever. And if I had to make a $50 bet, I bet that cab driver will, too.

TEN CENTS ON THE DOLLAR

Stepping out of the cab in Toronto, my foot nudged something on the ground. I bent over to investigate. There, lodged halfway under the passenger seat, I discovered a leather wallet. I thanked the driver, grabbed the wallet and my suitcase, and closed the taxi door behind me.

Once I checked into the hotel and found my room, I took the opportunity to investigate my finding. Whoever owned this wallet was doing pretty well for himself. Even before I opened the fold, I admired the even stitches, burnished edges, and the subtle embossed logo. The inside of the wallet confirmed my suspicions. In addition to credit cards and a stack of identical business cards, I found $1,000 in Canadian bills and around $600 or $700 in U.S. exchange.

A slow whistle slipped past my teeth. I hadn't held this much cash outside a Monopoly game.

I pocketed the wallet and my room key before heading to the lobby pay phone I'd spotted earlier. No one was using it. Pulling out the wallet, I took one of the business cards and lifted the receiver. I called collect, pushing in the number listed on the card when prompted.

A woman answered. "I'm sorry, we don't accept collect calls."

"Wait a minute. This is important," I said in a rush. "I found someone's wallet."

I held my breath, waiting for the dial tone, sure she'd cut me off. Instead, after a slight pause, she accepted the call. "You found a wallet?" she confirmed.

"Yes, in a taxi. And I found this number on a business card inside."

"This is great news," she said. "He's been looking all over for it."

"Well, if he wants, he can call me back." I gave her the number of the pay phone and hung up. Proud of my good deed, I started to walk away. Well, crap. I couldn't wander too far away from the phone. No doubt I looked like a wind-up toy on the wrong path, stopping and turning again with no real direction.

Fortunately, that's when the phone rang.

"Hello?"

"I hear you found my wallet," said a man's voice.

"Yes sir," I said.

"Thank you so much. You don't know how much it means to me. I'm going to send one of my employees over right now to get it. Can you wait?"

"Sure, how long will it be?" I asked.

The man confirmed my address. "We're close by," he

said. "It'll just be a few minutes."

"Okay," I agreed. "I'll wait for him."

We were just about to hang up, when something occurred to me. "Hey, wait a minute," I said.

"Yes?"

"Let me tell you what's in this wallet since I'm handing it over to someone other than you."

"Sure," he said. "That's a good idea."

I told him about the credit cards, business cards, and what looked like a house key. "There's also a stack of Canadian bills and a stack of U.S. bills."

"That sounds right."

I confirmed the amounts with him, and he said everything was just as he'd left it.

"I'm going to slip one of my business cards in here," I told him. "That way if you have any questions, you can get a hold of me."

"Great. Again, thank you."

We hung up and true to his word, a man showed up just a few minutes later. He identified himself, took the wallet, and left.

I didn't think much more about the incident until a few weeks later when I received an envelope in the mail with a Canadian postal code. Inside was a gift certificate for a hundred dollars as well as a personalized note from the wallet owner.

Dear Mr. Osborn, I truly appreciate you taking the time to return my wallet. It means a lot. I'm especially grateful that we had the chance to go over its contents, as I later realized the cash was missing when my employee returned it to me. Given the circumstances, he is no longer with my company. Thank you again for your honesty and kindness. Wishing you all the best.

I set the card and envelope aside.

Oh man.

Instead of feeling righteous about my honesty—joy that justice had been served—my first thought was, *I totally could have gotten away with it.*

I'd had the perfect patsy. I could have pocketed the cash and let the poor guy take the fall. I mean, how did the wallet owner know I wasn't the real thief? For all he knew, I was rolling in Canadian cash, sipping an overpriced hotel bar cocktail, and toasting my own cleverness.

I shook my head and laughed, slipping the gift certificate into my wallet. Well, at least I learned the price of honesty was about ten cents on the dollar.

IF AT FIRST YOU DON'T SUCCEED, CRASH THE YACHT AGAIN

I almost added yacht captain to my resume.

My friend, John Wooden, worked for a guy so rich he didn't even have a concept of money. This guy, we'll call him Richie, swam in dollar bills in his mother's womb and when he was born, the nannies wiped his butt with fivers. He could send you to buy a McDonald's hamburger, and when he asked you how much it cost, you could tell him $500, and he'd hand over five crisp Benjamins without a second thought.

Being born into money, Richie grew up to make even more. His business ventures were successful and pushed him into a tax bracket only known to few. After he'd filled his swimming pool to the top with all his extra cash and still had some to spare, he did what so many rich men had done before him. He bought a status symbol.

John worked for Richie as a pilot. But when Richie bought a huge, beautiful beast of a yacht up in New York City, he asked John to sail it down to Florida. Now there was nothing John couldn't do. He'd been a fighter pilot in Vietnam and was a tough-as-steel Marine. He wasn't a big man, but I don't know any three guys in the world who could take him, and John was always ready for a good fight. Once you got to know him, you'd learn he was actually a teddy bear, but you still wouldn't want to fight him.

While John could fly anything with wings, sailing was another story. I'm not sure John had ever stepped foot on a yacht before Richie asked him to park his boat down in Florida, but that didn't stop John from accepting the job. He was the type of guy who'd try anything, and if he could fly an airplane in Vietnam in the midst of oncoming enemy fire, how hard could it be to sail a yacht in calm waters?

So John and his wife Connie headed to the Big Apple and found the yacht parked in the slip with all the other rich people's boats. For some, there aren't many opportunities to sail a yacht, so why not make a vacation out of it? After exploring the fancy ship with its expansive master suite, state-of-the-art entertainment system, and luxurious leather couches, John turned to the practicalities of actually sailing the thing. Despite the fancy-pants amenities, the only navigation equipment on board was a compass. He reasoned he'd get the yacht out into the ocean and stay within sight of the coastline.

Without too much trouble, John figured out how to back the ship out of the slip, and once far enough out, he pointed the boat south. The couple planned to keep the ship moving twenty-four hours a day, taking turns at the helm while the other slept. The nights were especially difficult, because in the darkness, the shoreline was no longer visible, but John made sure the compass pointed to Florida.

A couple of small storms and bitterly cold nights later, they finally hit warmer air. Somewhere off the coast of South Carolina, John started to get cocky. He'd been right. Sailing a yacht was about the easiest thing a person could do. In fact, he was probably born to sail the seven seas. No doubt he could operate a yacht as well as any seaman.

At last, they reached the jutting peninsula, home of white-sand beaches, man-eating alligators, and some of the fanciest yacht docking in the United States. John masterfully sailed the behemoth into the bay and spotted the slip where the yacht was to be parked.

For the past four days, John only sailed the ship in one direction—straight. But he couldn't continue in a straight line and park the yacht. He was going to have to turn. Maneuvering a yacht isn't like driving a car, or even like handling the controls of an airplane. A plane responds immediately to light touches on the control yoke. A yacht carries a bit more inertia. Turning a yacht's tiller doesn't result in immediate results. A sailor can cut the throttle, but there's no button to turn off the ocean. A person must decide to stop long before he wants the yacht to quit moving.

Of course, this was information John didn't have.

Big expensive yachts were parked on either side of the empty slip. On one, a party was in full-swing. Privileged people in prestigious frocks peacocked along the deck. A few gazed out with upturned looks of surprise to see a boat heading straight towards them.

John felt the heat of Florida glare down on him. Drenched in sweat, he yanked at the tiller like a man trying to wrestle an alligator in a tuxedo. The yacht, unimpressed, continued its stately march toward destruction.

With all the grace of a drunken walrus, the yacht careened into the party boat, sending champagne flutes, and a few party-goers, overboard. One particular woman buoyantly floated near the dock, screaming, "Save me! Save me!"

Once the passengers were rescued, the owner of the damaged yacht was ready to discuss the situation. Instead of a conversation, John handed over Richie's credit card. "I think this should take care of it," he said.

A few years later, Richie bought a bigger and better yacht, and John crashed that one, too. "After that, I figured it out," John said. "I was taking the yacht to the Bahamas all by myself. It took a while, but after crashing two yachts, I figured it out and I got pretty good at it."

It was around this time the rules changed. In order to operate a yacht, someone on-board needed to have their Hundred-Ton Captain's license. This seemed like a pretty good rule, considering the foibles of John's yacht troubles. Since I was between airline jobs, John asked if I'd be willing to train in Fort Lauderdale and add seafaring to my resumé.

It wasn't going to be on my dime, so I thought, why not?

At that point, I hadn't run anything bigger than a ski boat on the Missouri River, but like John, I was pretty certain I could figure out how to navigate the seas as well as I could navigate the clouds. To prepare for school, John invited me down to the Ozarks to play around with Richie's 40-foot cabin cruiser. I didn't want to show up at captain's school like some clownfish, so I did my best to pay attention to John's instructions. He thought a good teaching method was for us to bar hop from dock to dock. I've never been good at holding my alcohol, so I never got too good with the boat.

Though I was scheduled to attend captain's school, I never sat through a day in class. Richie's yacht deal fell through, so I remained a bird in the sky instead of a fish out of water.

And honestly, I think that's just as well—even though "almost yacht captain" has a nice ring to it. I've always believed in saying yes to an adventure—even if it means crashing a few things along the way. But between the open sea and the open sky, I guess I just knew where I belonged.

WHAT DIDN'T GO WRONG

"Any interest in a quick, easy job that'll make you a decent amount of money?" Bill asked.

"You had me at easy," I said. "And money."

Bill flew a Leer 45 for a corporation that could bankroll a small country and still own yachts. The job was simple enough. Fly the big wig of the corporation and his wife to Grand Junction, Colorado, hang out a few days on the guy's property, and then fly back home. What could go wrong?

Bill introduced me to our passengers, Hank and Rosaline. Hank had a firm grip, the type you'd expect from the head of a multi-million-dollar corporation, but when I went to pull my hand away, he held tight. "Now, are you going to bitch about staying in the lodge like the other pilot did?"

Immediately my mind swirled at what I might have gotten myself into, but I was quick with an answer. "I can't imagine I'd bitch about staying in a lodge, sir."

"Good," he said, finally releasing my hand. "Because

pilots are a dime a dozen, good ranch hands are hard to find."

I laughed, and we immediately hit it off.

The flight to Grand Junction was unremarkable, but I still remember the drive through the mountains to the property. It was late-fall, but already the ground was thick with fluffy white snow, so pretty and perfect it looked strategically placed like part of a movie set. The sun illuminated tiny ice crystals in the white blankets, which contrasted against the jutting red peaks. The heavy branches of the Colorado Spruce trees glistened silver.

We pulled into the entrance of the property where we could see the maintenance facility and the houses where the workers lived. The burly ranch manager introduced himself as *Gus* and gave us a tour. He showed us two beautiful cabins, each with two bedrooms, private bathrooms, and fully stocked kitchens. There was no lodge in sight, but I didn't have a chance to ask about it.

"Hey, how about everyone comes to our house for dinner?" Hank suggested.

"As long as I don't have to wear a tie, I'm always available for a free meal," I said.

Hank laughed and slapped me on the back. "Great, see you in a few hours."

So there we were in Hank and Rosaline's house enjoying nice, casual conversation. If you didn't know Hank was a billionaire a million times over, you'd never guess it. He stood over his massive custom-built luxury stove, with its polished metal finishes, that held elk he'd shot himself and with a level of expertise indicating this wasn't his first time in a kitchen. The side dishes were natural ingredients, many procured from the land, the simplicity of the meal adding to its exquisiteness.

Not being a guy who notices details like women's clothing and jewelry, I might not have paid attention to Rosaline's earrings, except she kept tugging on her left ear. Like the home-cooked meal, these earrings were understated in their elegance. Delicate filigree gold wrapped around shimmering gems, giving them a deceivingly simple appearance.

Finally, she removed the earring. "I'm sorry," she said. "This thing has been bothering me all day."

Laying it on the table, the conversation continued, but I couldn't stop staring at the earring. I couldn't have cared less what it looked like. I can't even remember what color the gems were. What caught my attention was the obviously bent clasp. A Leatherman multi-tool sat on the counter, and before I could think twice about what I was doing, I had both the tool and the earring in my hand.

So consumed in making this relatively easy repair, I didn't notice all the eyes at the table centered on me. I took the tool, bent the earring a little bit so the hook could function properly, and handed the earring back to her. "There, that should work."

"Oh," she said, taking the earring and slipping it through her lobe, "it feels perfect now!"

I felt Hank's gaze on me. He gave a little chuckle. "Do you have any idea how much that earring you just bent is worth?"

I swallowed the elk in my mouth. "I'm not sure, but probably more money than I'll ever make in my life."

"Yeah, you're pretty close."

"Well, it works," Rosaline said. "I can wear it now."

The evening continued, and I didn't think too much about how close I'd flown to the danger zone. We thanked Hank and Rosaline for their company, and Bill drove us back to the cabins. "These cabins are pretty big," Bill said. "You can stay in your own if you'd like, or we can share one."

"I'm fine with sharing."

As Bill got settled, I built a fire outside. I still wondered about the mysterious lodge Hank mentioned. Likely these cabins were the lodge, and Hank and I simply had different definitions of the word. When you were as rich as Hank, you could call things pretty much whatever you wanted, and no one was going to argue with you.

"This is a beautiful lodge," I told Bill once he joined me around the fire. "I can't believe anyone would complain about this."

"Oh this isn't the lodge," Bill said. "The lodge is up the road." He gestured casually towards the dark. "Normally we'd have stayed there tonight, but it got too late. You can head there tomorrow."

"Okay."

I told myself I had no reason to be nervous.

Bill told me his plans to take advantage of the slopes for the next couple of days. "You can come if you want," he said.

"I'd love to come, but my knees aren't interested."

"You okay with being on your own for a couple of days?"

"Of course." As much as I enjoy people, I could contentedly live out my days as a hermit. There's something freeing about only having yourself to make happy.

"In the morning, take the Sno-Cat up to the lodge and stay there. It'll be fully stocked and ready for you," Bill said.

"Alright, I'll do that."

The mention of a Sno-Cat excited me. I'd always wanted to play around with one, but they weren't in my budget. The machines were famously employed in the first overland crossing of Antarctica in the 1950s, and were popular for arctic expeditions. Apparently they were also a fun plaything for the super-rich. Since some models were more expensive than the average American home, I figured this might be my only chance to drive one around.

In the morning, as Bill headed to the rental car, I followed him out and waved him off. "Hey, by the way, where is this lodge?" I called.

"Oh, up that way," he said, motioning towards the white expanse. "Just go straight, you can't miss it."

Bill's rear-view lights were still within sight when I tossed my suitcase in the Sno-Cat. I couldn't wait to get my hands on this machine, assuming I could figure out how to turn it on. It couldn't be that difficult. I'd operated $400 million-dollar jets, $80,000 luxury cars, a couple of motorboats, and several tractor models. I knew my way around machinery. There was no way I'd let this $200,000 piece of equipment intimidate me.

Within seconds, I located the key, already inserted in the ignition, and twisted it clockwise. The engine roared to life and I felt the machine's power vibrate beneath me. This was going to be fun. Unlike a car, or tractor, or even an airplane, a Sno-Cat doesn't have wheels. It operates on tracks which pull the vehicle forward, helping it to navigate steep, icy terrains and deep, snowy conditions. I studied the dashboard filled with all sorts of buttons, gauges, hydraulic controls, and a joystick. I half-heartedly looked around for a control manual. Not that I would have read it, because directions are for quitters. Still, in a worst-case scenario, it might be good to have on-hand. Seeing none, I started pushing buttons, experimenting with the controls, discovering this was actually a fairly complex piece of machinery.

Did I mention I was a pilot? I'd made a career out of complex machinery. If arctic explorers and scientists could run these machines, I'd have no problem.

The sun had been up for an hour or so, and the snow reflected the soft glow of early morning. I almost hated to mark the pristine frosted hills with the tracks of the Sno-Cat, but once I figured out the difference between forward and reverse, I had that baby crawling up the hill as easily as gliding across a skating rink. When I crested the hill, I caught my first glimpse of the lodge. I realized it'd been silly to confuse the cozy cabins with the lodge. Though still a distance away, I recognized the lodge as a giant, and I felt a little bit like Jack and the Beanstalk. It was this huge, imposing, hotel-like structure, like a castle from one of those Disney movies, specifically the ones where the princesses are held captive until they develop Stockholm Syndrome.

I navigated towards it, across the frozen tundra, just enjoying the hell out of that Sno-Cat, playing around with it and having the best time. Meanwhile, the lodge loomed bigger and bigger. Each time I caught a glimpse, it doubled in size. I drove right up to the front door, parked the Sno-Cat, and grabbed my bag. I stood looking up at the building like I was a termite asking to be let in.

I knocked on the door even though Bill had said no one would be there; predictably, no one answered. I opened the heavy door to a massive entryway. "Hello?" I called, not expecting an answer, but feeling like someone must be watching me. That's when I saw all the eyes. The lobby walls were covered with hunting trophies—antelope, elk, bear, bobcats, and other exotic animals with acrylic, unwavering eyes followed my echoing footsteps as I moved through the lobby and into a hallway.

Bill instructed me I wasn't to enter any of the locked bedrooms, but all the other rooms were fair game. It crossed my mind. What was behind those locked doors? Or maybe who? I decided it was best to block any of those thoughts from my mind and just walk past the rooms whose doorknobs didn't turn.

In my career, I've seen some impressive things. I've stayed in some very nice hotels. I've had plenty of all-expense paid travel experiences. This was something else. The lodge must have contained at least twenty bedrooms, each with a private bath and a hot tub on a balcony overlooking the Rocky Mountains. You could have ridden a dirt bike from one end of the building to the other and hit all five gears. In my wanderings, I discovered a game room with everything from pinball machines to shooting galleries—any game you could imagine. Since this was a hunting lodge, the building was outfitted with stations where you could come in, take off your gear, and hang up your guns. I discovered a commercial kitchen with every modern convenience imaginable, and next to the kitchen was a big observation area with curved glass windows and a 270 –degree-view of the mountains. And that was just the first floor.

Upstairs I found more bedrooms, a smaller commercial kitchen, and plenty of art and knickknacks that could likely fund a person's retirement. The lodge was stocked with every amenity needed or imagined.

I chose a bedroom, tossed my bag on the luggage stand like a civilized person, and soaked in one of the most beautiful hot tubs I'd ever seen. The air was freezing. I could feel ice specks in my nose with each inhale. The water burned deliciously against my skin and plumes of steam rose from the water. High up on the balcony with only the mountains and hardy trees for company, I felt like the only person left in the world. Beyond the jets of the hot tub, the world was silent, all sounds absorbed in the dense snow.

After my muscles melted into relaxation and my hands and feet turned pruney, I decided it was time to cook dinner.

I headed downstairs to the larger of the two

professional-grade kitchens. The fridge was loaded with fresh produce, beer, cheese, and condiments. The deep freeze was stuffed to the brim with meats and seafoods of every variety. There was no way the pantry had been organized by a man, considering the neat rows of spices, oils, and dry ingredients labeled into clear glass jars. There was even a special appliance in the kitchen dedicated to thawing foods safely at the most optimal temperatures. I'd never died from throwing ground beef in the sink overnight to thaw, but what the heck? I pawed through the thawing drawer, my eyes growing bigger with each more impressive and expensive cut of meat. Once or twice, I paused, looking all around the kitchen to be sure there weren't hidden cameras somewhere. Surely this was too good to be true. It wasn't possible I'd been turned loose with this much decadence. Maybe I'd go easy, just in case someone was watching.

Then I stumbled across the biggest bone-in ribeye I'd ever seen in my life. Marked as three and three-quarters pounds, the package listed the beef as Wagyu, dry-aged for 120 days. To hell with moderation, I thought, tearing open the white packaging to reveal intense marbling throughout the meat. If someone watched through hidden cameras, they were about to watch an unrivaled gorging.

I grabbed the beef, a large russet potato from the pantry, and set about chopping and steaming fresh vegetables, baking the potato in the oven, and searing the steak over the indoor grill. My mouth watered as the fats of the ribeye popped and sizzled, the smell filling the kitchen while the grill's hood sucked the smoke into the star-filled Colorado sky.

When I stumbled across a chocolate cake mix in the pantry, I thought, *why not?* As the smell of rich, sweet chocolate filled the air, I stuffed my mouth full of ribeye, and briefly wondered if I was in the adult version of Hansel and Gretel. Surely a witch watched somewhere nearby, waiting until the button on my pants broke loose and clattered across the porcelain marble floor, signaling my waistline had reached new epic proportions. She'd bide her time until I was in the throes of meat sweats, whipped cream smeared across my face, my happiness levels maxed to the point where I didn't care if she wanted to throw me in an oven and eat me.

The house bore an eerie silencer. As much as I loved to be alone, part of me kept waiting for someone to chop through the door and yell, "Heeeeeeeeeeeeeeere's Johnny!"

Yet, the evening wore on and soon I was too tired to think about witches or intruders. I stumbled in my bed past dark-o'clock, sunk under the covers, and drifted into a long, peaceful food coma.

The next morning, a beam of translucent Colorado light poured over my face. I awoke still stuffed from the night before. I lay there awhile, thinking of the other pilot Hank mentioned, the one who'd bitched about the lodge. What had he experienced that I had not? Was there something strange going on I hadn't recognized?

There I was, alone in a lodge built for 40 people, filled with enough food to generously feed thirty, a Sno-Cat at my disposal, hot tubs on every balcony, and absolutely no one else's wishes to grant. What was the catch? I'd seen *Beauty and the Beast* with my kids. There were hidden dangers within an enchanted castle. My mind wandered to the locked doors, the taxidermy trophies, some with mouths permanently forming silent screams. I almost jumped out of my bed when the familiar guitar strum of my cellphone signaled an incoming call from Bill.

"Everything okay?" he asked.

"Yep. No problems here."

"Glad to hear it. Let's plan to meet back at the cabins tomorrow at two."

"Alright. Works for me."

"You sure everything is fine?" he asked.

I sat up in my bed, grabbed the shirt I'd tossed on the floor the night before. "Is there any reason it wouldn't be?"

"Not that I can think of," he said.

"Well, thanks for checking in. You have yourself a good day."

"Thanks Don, you too."

The phone beeped and again the house retreated into absolute silence.

I threw on my outer clothes and went outside to breathe in the fresh air, which was as clear and sharp as glass. The Sno-Cat roared to life with an easy turn of the ignition, and I was off again, testing the vehicle's ability to surmount the sides of steep cliffs, testing its handling on the downhill slopes, checking its maneuverability in the deepest drifts.

It felt like a dream—like I'd been thrown into a perfect snow globe. As much fun as I was having, something niggled at me. How long until something came along and shook the hell out of this slice of paradise? What hidden disaster hovered nearby, turning this place from bliss to something to bitch about?

I suppressed the worry as much as possible and experienced moments of transcendence, like when I watched a bald eagle soar against the cerulean sky, came upon a herd of white-tailed deer biting at long wisps of grass protruding through the snow, and stopped to watch a river burble under a layer of ice.

But the feeling of unease followed me back to the lodge. Outside, darkness intruded upon the shortening daylight hours. Again I called out when I entered the lobby, hearing only the echo of my own voice. I felt the eyes of the long-dead animals follow me down the endless corridors to the kitchen.

Doubt started to creep in. What if this place wasn't what it seemed? What if the locked rooms contained the bodies of former pilots? What if I wasn't in the right place after all, and I was going to be prosecuted for breaking and entering? Maybe I'd forgotten to apply the parking brake on the Sno-Cat and at any moment it would come crashing through the heavy doors. Perhaps the apocalypse had shut down civilization and the only remaining survivors were me and a murderous cannibal who'd sneak into my room late that night.

I didn't plan on dying on an empty stomach. That night I cooked lobster, scallops, and little shrimp and served it with a spicy cocktail sauce. I sautéed finely shredded cabbage in leftover bacon grease with a splash of apple cider vinegar and salt. I finished off the chocolate cake in big, greedy mouthfuls. If anyone ever lived like a king, it was me for that day-and-a-half at the lodge in Grand Junction, Colorado. If I was going to be murdered in my sleep or tossed in the oven by an evil witch, by God it had been worth it.

The next morning, I awoke very much alive and not murdered. I enjoyed one last soak in the hot tub, my breath visible and carrying up a silent prayer of thankfulness to the highest of the mountain peaks. I enjoyed another hearty breakfast, and did my best to leave the kitchen looking presentable. I packed my bag, tossed it in the Sno-Cat, and drove down the hillside. Was this when the avalanche would crush me under its power? Would this be the moment Big Foot revealed his existence?

I spotted Bill's truck by the cozy cabins. He waved a greeting and I parked the Sno-Cat, now an expert in its handling. "How was it?" he asked.

"Good," I said.

"Good," he said.

I hopped in the passenger seat and Bill told me about his ski trip while we drove to the airport. We flew back to Omaha, landed safely, and that night I slept in my own bed. Nothing bad happened at all.

I'd lived like a king, like an emperor who ruled over a winter wonderland. So much hadn't gone wrong. Yet, I'd wasted some of those precious hours on-edge, waiting for the other shoe to drop. I had to wonder. Wouldn't it be better to enjoy each moment rather than spending all day worrying about something that turned out to be a non-event? If it's impossible to live your life in reverse, why live it in fast forward? Better to take each moment as it comes, and be thankful for each one that doesn't go wrong.

BLEEPING RICH

They say friends can't be bought, but this didn't stop Kel from trying. He had more dollars than sense and even less charm. I felt a little sorry for him. He longed for companionship, but no amount of money made his personality more appealing.

But he did own a helicopter.

I met him by-chance at the Millard Airport in Omaha. A friend of mine introduced us. At the time I had no idea who Kel was or how much money he had. I did wonder if I'd have to wash my ears out with soap after listening to him talk.

"Holy bleep," he said. "Are you a helicopter pilot too?" he asked me.

"I've got a few hours logged," I admitted. "But the expense of getting the license didn't make sense for my situation."

"So what do you fly?"

"About everything else besides helicopters—commercial jets, planes, the occasional hang glider."

"No bleep?"

"Yep."

"But you like helicopters?" he asked.

"Sure."

"I thought you might. You don't strike me as a total idiot."

"Thanks," I said. "I appreciate that."

"Hey, I'm flying to my property over by Norfolk next week. If you're free, you can come along. A man of the sky like yourself deserves a real bleeping flight. Planes are fine if you like autopilot."

A man of lesser maturity might have taken offense to a comment like that. But I was willing to tolerate a walking wallet in exchange for a free helicopter ride. "Sounds great."

The next week we were back at Millard Airport. My seatbelt was secured and the rotors were spooling up.

"Airplanes are great," Kel said through my headset, "if you like needing a runway to get anywhere."

"Yeah, that's a good one." Could I turn the headset off, claim it had malfunctioned? But Kel probably had a backup on-board. Maybe two.

"I don't give a flying bleep what anyone says. Nothing beats this feeling."

The rotors hit full RPM, the helicopter beat the air into submission and rose into the sky. Outside my window, eastern Nebraska stretched out below me. I briefly caught sight of the Missouri River to the east before Kel navigated westward towards Norfolk. The scenery morphed from urban Omaha sprawl, to occasional tree canopies, to patchwork farmland.

"Mother bleeper, you're basically a glorified bus driver," Kel said.

"Excuse me?"

"A bus driver," he said again. "Only instead of driving passengers around on roads, you transport them in the sky."

"I guess I've never thought of that before." In truth, I had thought of it. I'd even made the same joke myself, but it was funny when I said it.

"That's the problem with those damn planes. They're built for passengers." Kel tapped his instrument panel. "Helicopters are built for missions."

"You aren't kidding."

"I am as serious as a bleeping heart attack."

Kel spent the next forty-five minutes in a steady stream of conversation, mostly about himself. He didn't require much from me, so I supplied the occasional 'uh huh' and 'you don't say.' Even the exhilaration of a helicopter ride couldn't overcome the exhaustion I felt in this man's company.

Still, I tried to be polite. No sense pissing off the guy who's got your life in his hands.

"It's right up ahead," Kel said sometime later. "Bleeping-A, would you look at that."

I followed his gaze. "Is that a resort?"

Kel laughed. "Kinda looks like one from up here, doesn't it? But it's just a little man cave helicopter pad."

"Holy bleep," I said. It wasn't like me to cuss, but an hour in Kel's company would put the pope in purgatory.

The closer we got to the property, the bigger it got. The chopper hovered for a moment, then Kel bumped the bird on the ground. I sat in stunned silence as the rotors slowed and the roar of the engine quieted enough to remove my earphones.

"For bleep's sake, don't just sit there. Come see Kel's Cave."

Despite myself, I was excited. Though I've never lived the lifestyle of the rich and famous, I never turned down a chance to visit. Kel played the role of the foul-mouthed tour guide, and I tried to keep my mouth from falling open as I saw each new feature of the property. The little man cave had a full-sized basketball court, a bar stocked with liquor I'd only seen in magazines, and a living area Kel referred to as his apartment, which was bigger than any house I'd ever lived in. It had all the amenities.

"What do you think?" he asked.

"Wow. It's beautiful." Kel's property was the kind of place that made you question every life decision you'd ever made—but only until you remembered the man who owned it.

He nodded. "It's nice enough, if I do say so myself."

We passed a few hours enjoying the property, and then Kel got a phone call.

"Hello? . . . You want O'Douls? Who the bleep drinks

O'Douls? . . . Fine, I'll stop by and pick some up. See you in a bit." He hung up the phone. "Time to get back. I just have to make a pit stop on the way."

I climbed in the helicopter, and soon we were back in the air.

"Bleeping bleep, would you get a load of this?" Kel swooped down over a rustic cabin by a river. "You see that?"

Down below sat a simple structure. It had four walls, a roof, likely only space inside for the bare necessities. It wasn't fancy, but well-kept. Seemed like someone cared enough to stop nature from taking it over.

"The cabin? Yeah, I see it."

"Piece of bleep, isn't it?"

"I don't know. Looks fine to me."

"The son of a bleep who lives there?"

The fragment hung in the air like a question. "Yeah, what about him?"

"That bastard is happier than I'll ever be." For the first time, Kel went quiet. The roar of the rotors filled the silence between us, but I could feel the weight of his words hanging in the air. I wanted to say something, but what do you tell a man with everything who still feels empty?

The cabin moved out of sight, but the image stayed with me. It was the opposite of Kel's man cave. There wasn't even room to land a helicopter. Yet it seemed like the type of place a person might find happiness.

Kel soon found a fresh rant about something or another. But when he glanced out the window again, I caught something in his face—a flicker of longing, maybe even envy.

For all his money, I realized he was still searching for something he couldn't buy.

The guy was a bleep-hole. It wasn't a mystery why he didn't have a lot of friends. But for all his failings, I had to admit: Kel had some introspection.

We arrived back in Omaha, and I assumed Kel would drop me off at the airport where I'd left my car, but instead he landed his helicopter in an empty parking lot near a bar. "I'll be right back," he shouted. Leaving the helicopter idling, he abandoned me, and ran wind-swept into the building. He reappeared with a six-pack of O'Douls non-alcoholic beer.

"One more stop," he said, before I could ask.

A few minutes later we landed in the parking lot of a business. I had no idea what the rules were about helicopter parking in suburban areas, but I suppose with enough money, everything is legal. Having little choice in the matter, I followed him inside, where he handed over the drinks. By this time, several employees came out to see the helicopter in the parking lot. Kel seemed to know everyone. Soon he was getting requests for helicopter rides.

"Do you mind?" he asked, but I could tell my answer wouldn't matter.

I pictured my cheap car sitting at the airport. I imagined my fixer-upper house. I longed for the comfort of being back where I belonged. I saw the line forming by the helicopter, and the gleam in Kel's eyes. These people wanted him.

Perhaps only for a time, and maybe only for his helicopter; but for right now, they were his shiny new possessions. I'd been tossed aside like an old sock.

"Hey Mark," Kel yelled. "Give Don a ride back to his bleeping car, will ya?"

THE BIGGEST 25 CENT MISTAKE

We walked the Denver streets for hours. It was late fall, but one of those days they called *Indian Summer*, and we shed our jackets back at the hotel. Thirty hours was a lot of time to kill for a couple of airline pilots, so Bob Hemingway and I made the most of it, popping into different restaurants and stores, playing tourists as a welcome alternative to staring at the mass-produced art on the four walls of our rooms at the Sheraton.

This was back when airlines flew in and out of the old Stapleton Airport near downtown Denver, before the behemoth Denver International Airport closed Stapleton, and before the terminals and runways were repurposed into what is now called Central Park. Back then it was an easy walk from the airport hotels to downtown, and it was a nice day to stretch our legs after so many hours in the sky.

But now our legs were good and stretched. We'd been on our feet all day, walking up and down the Denver streets, and it was time to return to our hotel. "How about we catch one of those city buses," Bob suggested. "It'll drop us off right in front of the Sheraton."

"Sounds good to me."

We waited a few minutes at the next stop, and when the bus halted in front of us, we boarded the near empty vehicle and took seats adjacent to each other across the aisle. The bus rumbled along, and we were each quiet, lost in our own thoughts. The bus stopped. A new passenger stepped aboard. Bob smirked. Our thoughts synced. The man who entered through the bi-fold doors was one we wouldn't soon forget.

You couldn't miss the guy, let alone forget him. He looked like a giant banana or a walking yellow Slip 'N Slide.

Though he could have sat anywhere in the vacant bus, the man walked straight to the back and took the seat right in front of Bob. He was a well-kept gentleman, clean with combed-hair. But no one paid attention to his face, because there was no getting past his yellow suit. Strange, plastic, and bright enough to be spotted from the sky, his suit was tailored to his exact measurements. Someone had spent significant time sewing this outfit to precise specifications. In fact, I'd have described them as solid, good-looking clothes if they weren't bright yellow and plastic. Bob scooted back into his seat as though avoiding the plague.

I watched the man out of the corner of my eye, trying not to be too obvious, but this dude was anything but normal. He seemed disoriented and confused; but more than anything, he seemed curious, looking around and taking things in, as though he were seeing the inside of a city bus for the first time.

After a bit he turned around in his seat. "I need one of your twenty-five cent pieces," he said to Bob.

Of course, in a world accustomed to beggars, Bob and I did the thing where we pretended not to hear him, instead turning our attention to watching Denver blur by through the windows. This time he turned to me. "Is there any way you can let me have a twenty-five cent coin?"

I shook my head, thinking it a weird way to ask for a quarter. The man pulled out a sheet of notebook paper. "If you give me a twenty-five cent coin, I'll give you this paper."

I couldn't help it. He had my attention. "What's on it?" I asked.

He flashed it around. It had some sort of writing, but I couldn't decipher it from my side of the bus. "This is a formula," he said.

"Oh yeah?"

He dropped his voice to a whisper, even though we were the only ones on the bus. "It will allow you to pick the winning lottery numbers by listening to the compressor on your refrigerator."

I laughed. A formula based on fridge noises? "I think I'll pass," I told him.

Just then, the bus stopped at our hotel. Bob and I got off, careful to avoid eye contact with the man in the yellow plastic suit.

As the bus accelerated, I felt utter and total regret. "Bob, what the hell was on that piece of paper?"

My eyes tracked the bus. If it stopped, I'd make a run for it. Forget running, I might steal a bike and pedal after it. I'd give a quarter and buy his piece of paper. Heck, I'd give him a dollar. But the bus kept going, and I never saw him again.

"Why the hell didn't we buy it when we had a chance?" I asked Bob. "A measly twenty-five cents and I could have had it."

Bob laughed, likely assuming I was joking. "What planet was that guy from?" he asked.

"Not from around here, that's for sure."

We didn't say anything more about it, just ambled into our respective hotel rooms for the night.

Sleep didn't come easy. I couldn't get it out of my head. My fridge back home made all sorts of weird sounds—clicks, hums, occasional groans. Had I been ignoring financial success all these years? What if every pop and rattle had been whispering lottery numbers, just waiting for someone smart enough to listen? The more I thought about it, the more it gnawed at me. Was the man in the yellow plastic suit a lunatic… or a genius? Was he a visitor from somewhere else or some other time? Had he traveled from the future and needed to fuel his time machine with the specific metal properties in quarters? If he was from the future, he'd have studied our time, and he'd have known all the winning lottery numbers. If I had to do it over again, I would have given him a quarter.

Now, I'd like you to think I forgot about the man in the yellow plastic suit. And I'd like you to think I never once stood in front of my fridge at 2 a.m., head cocked, notebook in hand, straining to decipher its cryptic wisdom. That I didn't do it again the next night. Or the next week. That I don't still keep a notepad in the freezer in case the compressor has a sudden moment of clarity.

But the truth is sometimes more embarrassing than fiction. Listen, I know how it sounds. But if you ever hear a fridge compressor whispering numbers... promise me you'll write them down.

DRESS FOR SUCCESS

Peculiar things happen when I wear my flight uniform.

Random women hand me their crying babies. Strangers ask me for directions. Restaurant employees conspiratorially recommend I try the chicken and avoid the roast beef.

When I'm wearing my stained T-shirt and faded jeans and a day's growth of facial hair, those same people might cross the street should they see me coming.

But a pilot's uniform in an airport terminal turns you invincible, like Pac-Man after eating a power pellet. The crowded concourses open with clear passages, and I feel a bit like Moses parting the Red Sea. As I head to my gate, I feel gazes of admiration, envy, and respect, and all for simply walking to my job.

Walk through that same concourse in my tree-trimming shirt and all I get are elbows, bumped shoulders, and people in business suits cutting me off. There are no looks of admiration. Mostly I'm ignored. Though once in a while I think I spot a glance of pity, or from a more altruistic member of society, a concerned brow, wondering if they should intervene in helping what must be an addle-minded fool.

In my uniform, smiles are reciprocated. In my plain clothes, I get glares and clutched purses.

Sitting near a gate looking sharp in a neatly-pressed uniform, I watched as a husband and wife boldly approached. "Excuse me," the wife said. I looked up from my book. "Can you point us to Gate 38C?"

"Sure," I answered. "Turn around and go straight. It'll be right in front of you."

"Thank you so much," she said, all smiles and thankfulness.

As they were turning, I heard the husband whisper-yell, "That's exactly what I told you!"

"Well, since when do you ever know what you're talking about?" came the wife's reply.

No one approaches me for directions when I'm wearing gym shorts.

However, it's hard to get any peace at all when I'm in my flight gear. Usually I'll go out of my way to find an abandoned part of the airport, but invariably, someone will approach and say one of four things to me.

"Are you flying this thing out?"

"So, you have to wait around here just like the rest of us?"

"Where are you going today?"

Or

"Do you want to see me naked?"

One of the above statements might be a product of wishful thinking. But truly, there are things I can do in a uniform that would likely get me arrested in sweatpants. In an airport, I can motion for a little kid to come over and whisper something in his ear, and his mom is all grins. Do the same thing wearing a holey tee and security is escorting me out of the building.

The mother in scenario one can later be overheard telling her friends, "And the pilot even told Joey to be a good boy on the flight!" The mother in scenario two has a different tale. "Oh my God. This world is going to hell. Joey was almost abducted by a human trafficker right there in the Omaha airport!"

People seem genuinely interested in my opinions when I'm dressed for work. I get questions on everything: food, health, politics. My advice is appreciated and followed. But when I share my thoughts wearing jeans, Google receives a surge in searches for things like 'conspiracy theories' or 'how to diagnose a mental illness.'

Someday I think it would be a lot of fun to walk through a hospital wearing a white coat, or enter a hotel conference room wearing an expensive, tailored suit.

They say dress for the job you want. That's why I'll probably spend the rest of my days wearing cut-offs and a faded Spiderman shirt—a look that says *retired superhero who occasionally plays rock 'n' roll.* I'd be lying if I said I won't miss the accolades and respect, no matter how misdirected they may be, but I'm looking forward to growing my hair past regulation length. If people cross the street when they

see me coming, I'll just wave and enjoy the wide berth of
my own personal runway.

AFFIRMATION JUNKIE

There's no doubt my mom loved me. She loved me through acts of service. She loved me by putting my needs before her own. She loved me through self-sacrifice and by picking up the phone every time I called.

But she wasn't warm and fuzzy. She wasn't a hugger. She didn't spare unnecessary words. I don't have vivid memories of her saying, "I love you," or "I'm proud of you." I don't begrudge her this.

At least, not anymore.

We all love differently. Express our needs in unique ways. Mom didn't hand out affirmations like candy on Halloween. I could sense her love, but the words stuck in her mouth like taffy.

Part of me craved words of affirmation from Mom. Instead of "Good job, Don," I often heard about the one thing I did wrong. It didn't come from a place of meanness. Reading between the lines, I think the words meant something else entirely. Her critiques were the only way she could tell me how highly she thought of me. Because no matter how well I did, she knew I could do even better. She never wanted me to rest on good enough, because Mom wanted my best.

I didn't always have this level of understanding. And for years I craved affirmation like a kid with cavities craves sugar.

Affirmation wasn't to be found in the confines of Catholic school. There we followed strict dress codes, sat rigidly in class memorizing catechism, and recited prayers in-unison. Standing out invited ridicule. As a poor kid, I learned the rules quickly: don't be first, but don't be last.

Church followed the same pattern. Each week we sat in the same pew, at the same time. We sat, stood, knelt, prayed, and sang in a structured routine. Deviations disrupted devotion.

But high school was different. Without nuns enforcing every rule, the boundaries loosened—and so did I. I wasn't sure how to fit in, but I knew I wanted to be noticed—and on my own terms. I did start to stand out, but not in ways I hoped. My homemade clothing drew attention against my friends' simple jeans and pocket T-shirts. I drove beat-up clunkers or walked most places while other kids owned new cars. For the most part, it didn't bother me. But I yearned for recognition.

Then one day, I discovered something different. During speech class I made people laugh. The feeling sent electric jolts through my body. I felt a shift. A realization. What a phenomenal feeling to get a reaction, to know people were paying attention. Laughter proved the greatest form of affirmation. I wanted more.

Before long, I became the class clown.

That hunger for recognition didn't fade after high school—it just evolved. What started as cracking jokes in class turned into a love of performance, whether behind a microphone, in a cockpit, or on stage. I chased that same rush in every role I took on. That sense of performance carried me through life. The compulsion for positive feedback controlled me like a drug.

There's a joke in the airline industry: You never have to guess if someone is a pilot—they'll tell you within the first five minutes of meeting you. Now imagine what happens when that pilot publishes a book. I like to mention *Where We Land* in casual conversation, see if I can get a stranger to look it up on Amazon. And then the affirmation of watching someone add it to their cart is a small victory, but a meaningful one.

Affirmations change as you age. The ego settles. Maybe who I am is already enough. Maybe life is less about proving myself and more about enjoying what I have. Success and affirmation boil down to something as simple as waking up excited for the day, going to bed with a slight smile, finding joy in the little things—a workout, a podcast, a funny post from my sister.

I don't think I'm alone in seeking affirmation. It seems ingrained in the human spirit. Most of us have a desire to raise our hands and say, "Hey, I matter. I'm here."

Maybe that's why we have tombstones—to leave a mark, to say, "I was here. And maybe, just maybe, while I was here, I mattered."

*

"We got a book new review on Amazon," my sister, Annie, tells me over the phone.

"Oh yeah? What did it say?"

She reads me the words and I bask in a fuzzy glow.

"How cool is that?" I ask.

"Very cool."

"How often do you look at those reviews?" I'm curious.

"Probably more than I should. I'm a bit of an affirmation junkie," she admits.

I laugh. "Affirmation junkie. That would make a good book title."

"Maybe." She sounds doubtful.

"It'd be funny," I say. "But then people are going to ask which one of us is the affirmation junkie."

"Dang, you're right."

"And what will you say?" I ask.

"Honestly, we are probably both affirmation junkies," she says. "Must be something in our upbringing. But I'm happy to hide behind you on this one. Let you take the blame."

"Okay," I say. "I'll take the fall—but we both know the truth."

"Honestly, isn't everyone a little bit of an affirmation junkie?" Annie muses. "We all have a need to be noticed, to be recognized. I mean, it'd be better if we took all our satisfaction in just doing our best. But who doesn't like a little outside reassurance that what they do matters?"

"You know," I say. "I was thinking the exact same thing."

BIG DADDY GRUMPY BEAR

Once upon a time, there lived a Big Daddy Grumpy Bear.

There was no Mama Bear to tell him what to do, and no Baby Bear to cry about his porridge being the wrong temperature.

Big Daddy Grumpy Bear could eat his porridge at whatever damn temperature he wanted. And to be perfectly honest, he didn't even like porridge. He'd rather eat smoked ribs on his back patio.

Bears are known as opportunistic omnivores. Given the opportunity, they'll eat about anything. This bear was no exception. Anytime the Big Daddy Grumpy Bear was offered food, he'd say something along the lines of, "I can say no to anything but temptation."

Once there had been a Mama Bear and a couple of Baby Bears. When bears live together, there are compromises and expectations. All the bears work together to gather the berries, catch the salmon, and keep the doors locked at night. This is a particularly important step, because all bears know that Goldilocks the Freeloader always lurks nearby.

Goldilocks aside, there were happy times for the bear family: family vacations, water skiing on the river, fires in the backyard. The Baby Bears did lots of cute little bear things, and then they did more impressive Bigger Baby Bear things, and then all of a sudden they weren't Baby Bears anymore. They moved away to houses with door locks of their own, because a bear can never be too careful with someone like Goldilocks in the world.

The house was quiet with the Baby Bears gone, except when Big Daddy Grumpy Bear played his drum set. Or his electric guitar. In fact, those times were very loud. But when Big Daddy Grumpy Bear wasn't home, which was quite often, the house sat still and subdued. There were still expectations at home, still compromises that needed to be made. This is what bears do to make marriages work.

Sometimes, no matter how hard a bear tries, no matter how many salmon are brought home, there's just not enough honey left in the jar. These are sad times for bears. These are the times when some bears want to point fingers, and other bears want to blame themselves. But in these situations, it's everybody's fault and nobody's fault. Every effort can be made. Both Mama Bears and Daddy Bears can love each other, but still need separate houses with separate locks. Together or apart, bears must stay vigilant against Goldilocks.

So Big Daddy Grumpy Bear moved into his own house

with his own lock; and though he grieved the loss of what his family used to be, the bear harbored a secret. It wasn't much of a secret, because he told lots of other bears, but the truth was, Big Daddy Grumpy Bear liked living in his own house. He liked being able to play his drum set in the middle of the night or practice his electric guitar solo at full volume right after breakfast. He wasn't the type of bear to eschew compromises and expectations, but he rather liked living up to the expectations he set for himself.

While Big Daddy Grumpy Bear wasn't the materialistic sort, there were three things he'd always wanted, but had never been allowed to have. Now that he was no longer under the bearish obligation of compromise, he was ready to make some rather large purchases.

For years Big Daddy Grumpy Bear slept on a mattress that sagged in the middle. Each time he awoke from hibernation, he felt older and grumpier. True, he was older. And he certainly was grumpier. But he dreamt of a mattress that might help him feel young again. As a cub, he'd been able to fall asleep on any mattress at any time and wake up feeling powerful. These days he awoke feeling like someone had clobbered him with a sack of rocks in the middle of the night.

What Big Daddy Grumpy Bear needed was the perfect mattress. It wouldn't be too hard or too soft, but just right. It would provide superior comfort and pressure release. It wouldn't trap heat like a regular mattress, but rather be made from a scientifically-designed hyper-elastic grid for "the coolest, most comfortable, deepest sleep." Admittedly, the marketing team at The Purple Mattress Company knew what they were doing. Big Daddy Grumpy Bear bought a queen-size Purple mattress, which was not excessively big, nor cub-sized small, but just the right size.

And damn. The advertisements hadn't misled. Big Daddy Grumpy Bear slept as though he were floating on a Care Bear cloud. It was money well-spent.

Now that he was sleeping so well, Big Daddy Grumpy Bear was ready to make his next big purchase. He'd always wanted a hot tub. He could imagine himself soaking on his back deck. On frosty mornings, his breath would mingle with the steam, rising into the trees. Big Daddy Grumpy Bear would keep the tub at just the right temperature, not too hot and not too cold, but just right at 102 degrees.

The day the tub was installed felt like the first day of spring. Bears love the first day of spring. It's the day they come out of their carefully locked doors and break their winter fasts. It's the day they have carte blanche to eat all the fruits and fish they can find. They eat and eat and eat until the rumble of their winter bellies is a distant echo. Of course, Big Daddy Grumpy Bear preferred steak and spicy Thai food over fruits and fish, but it's the same basic idea.

Life with the hot tub was grand. Each morning, Big Daddy Grumpy Bear would rise out of his Purple mattress and walk straight to the hot tub in his underwear. A nice thing about living alone is there are no expectations that a bear wear anything but his underwear in a hot tub. Fortunately for the neighbors, there were still certain societal expectations he felt obliged to follow, such as the presumption that one should not appear bear-naked in the backyard.

Each morning he felt less and less grumpy as his aches, pains, and worries melted away in the perfectly programmed hydrotherapy spa jets.

Big Daddy Grumpy Bear had always been taught that money could not buy happiness. But he was beginning to have some doubts.

There was still one more big purchase to complete the trifecta.

Big Daddy Grumpy Bear wanted a massage chair. Now, he didn't want one of those lame-ass chairs that just jiggle and vibrate you until your skin itches. He didn't want one disguised as a normal recliner with a built-in heating pad and little gremlin hands that punched at you from the inside. He had his eye on the Massage Chair of all massage chairs. He set his sights on a chair that looked like some sort of advanced space technology. Some bears might call it an eye sore, but those bears wouldn't be invited to enjoy the personalized and health-conscious massage experience this machine had to offer.

The chair was so big it wouldn't fit through the front door. It had to be assembled right there in the living room. But once in place, it was just the right size.

But one thing was for sure. When Big Daddy Grumpy Bear was sitting in that chair having his calves, feet, forearms, neck, shoulders, and lower back simultaneously worked into smooth butter, he didn't give two cents how it looked. As far as he was concerned, it looked genius-level smart. Gone were his aches and pains and the cricks and cracks which previously prevented him from living the happiest of bear lives.

Nights on the Purple mattress followed by mornings in the hot tub left Big Daddy Grumpy Bear feeling like a spry cub. The massage chair felt like a cherry on top of a three-layered frosted cake, unnecessary, but delicious all the same. Life was good. He felt content in this solitary existence.

There were times he missed the growls of the Baby Bear cubs. He reminisced over the happier days of his marriage. It's a strange feeling bears can have, when they feel gladness and sorrow at the same time.

Now Big Daddy Grumpy Bear still traveled a fair bit, so he wasn't always at home to enjoy his three wondrous purchases. But each time he turned the key in the lock upon his return, it felt like a reunion amongst old friends.

One day, returning from a trip, Big Daddy Grumpy Bear noticed something unusual. Though he hadn't been home for several days, there was a fresh trail of water leading from the hot tub into the house. Concerned, he followed the trail. It led to a discarded, still-damp pair of swimming trunks. In his sink, he found a single, golden strand of hair. His own hair was black. Or at least mostly black, but those rogue silver strands were certainly not blond.

"Someone's been using my hot tub," he said.

Walking through the rest of the house, he stopped at his massage chair. The power button was on. He was always careful to turn the power button off.

"Someone's been using my massage chair," he said.

Next he went into his bedroom. His bed was still un-made. He'd set no expectations on himself to make his bed each morning when he'd unmake it again that night. The Purple mattress was divine whether or not the sheets were rumbled or straight.

"At least no one has been sleeping in my bed," he said. "Or at least as far as I can tell."

He eased himself onto the bed, immediately comforted by the responsive coils. He had some thinking to do. Someone had been in his hot tub. Someone had been in his massage chair. He'd found a golden strand of hair in his sink. All the evidence pointed to a singular suspect.

He knew exactly who to call.

"Hello?" said the voice on the other end.

"Have you been in my hot tub?" he asked.

"Yeah, I stopped over after work."

"Have you been in my massage chair?"

"Yep, I used that after the hot tub."

"Have you been on my Purple mattress?"

"No. Geez, Dad, why would I want to lay in your bed?"

"Okay, just checking. How was it?"

"The hot tub or the massage chair?"

"Either, both."

"Honestly? Pretty incredible. How did you know?"

"At first I was worried Goldilocks had gotten in, but then I found your swim trunks on my bathroom floor and you didn't turn off the power button on the massage chair."

"Oh damn, sorry about that," his son said.

"That's okay. You locked the door behind you, and

that's the most important thing."

"Of course. Gotta keep out Goldilocks."

"Alright, son, I'll talk to you later. The hot tub is calling."

Big Daddy Grumpy Bear ended the call and inhaled a deep breath of satisfaction. He loved using his hot tub. And he loved using his massage chair. But what gave him the most pleasure of all, is when he could share those gifts with others. At least, as long as they had a key and locked the door behind them.

Because a bear can never be too careful with someone like Goldilocks on the prowl.

ONE LAST PIG OUT

No one guessed a plate of frozen steaks could spark a tradition that would span forty years. The tradition would see hair come and go, pounds come and stay, and friendships solidify.

It started simple.

After a hot day of deck building, Mike Carson and Tom Ahrens needed a break. It was one of those oven-summer days, the type where stepping outside felt like becoming a loaf of bread baking in the middle rack—no breeze, only heat pressing in from all sides. They decided to rent a cabin out at Chadron State Park, where the temperature always hovers a few degrees cooler than town. But first they needed reinforcements.

Tom raided his cousin's freezer and helped himself to a stack of steaks. Mike loaded up on things from his mom's fridge. For the next two days, the friends did nothing but eat and relax.

They couldn't let a good thing be a one-time deal. The next year they invited a few more friends, and still more the year after that.

I accepted my invitation without hesitation.

We started calling it Pig-Out Weekend. Soon we were all raiding fridges. Though some of us actually went to the store to purchase food to contribute.

As it grew, it got more organized. One of the first rules was, "No women allowed." Then some of us started getting girlfriends. The rule evolved into, "Okay, you can bring women, but they have to be associated with you. No Dolly Parton look-alikes just because you can afford them."

Back then, the booze flowed faster than a combine chewing through a wheat field at harvest time—unstoppable, messy, and occasionally dangerous. We never worried about hangovers. At that age, we were young enough to outdrink the consequences.

But age and consequences play the long game. As we got older, a lot of us stopped drinking. Others became alcoholics and experienced the cure. So our gatherings became quieter and calmer, but somehow more satisfying.

The menu also evolved. What started out as a pile of steaks grew into an all-you-can-eat buffet of King Crab Legs, hot dogs, and everything in between, each plate a testament to how far we'd come. Some of the best food I've had in my life came from Pig-Out Weekend.

At one point, the weekend peaked with elaborate smokers and planned excursions, but I think we all liked it best when it morphed into, "let's just pull up a chair and be us for a while." Not many people have friends who trace back to childhood. Friends who know your past, your present, and all the dumb things you regret in between. You can't lie to an old friend. You can barely tell him what's new. And there's such a deep comfort in being known despite it all and accepted just the same.

We used to be a bunch of twenty year-olds fresh out of high school. Now we're grandpas with knee braces and heart meds. Some of us got married (a few too many times), some never settled down, and some aren't here anymore.

But some things haven't changed at all. No matter how long we've been apart, it only takes about ten seconds before the same old dynamic falls back into place. We tell the same stories and jokes we've been telling for twenty years, and somehow they just keep getting funnier.

Kenny Groves's cakes are another annual staple. Who can forget the giant boob cake? Now they usually come with tamer decor, with sayings like "Happy Pig Out Weekend," or "Don Made It This Year," after I missed a couple years in a row.

Tom, one of the original proprietors, keeps a worn journal with forty years of memories. Each year, the journal makes an appearance, and everyone is obliged to leave a memory before they leave. It's a treasure trove of our collected memories, a story told one line at a time, the entries all containing a similar theme—*same ol' shit: good food, good friends, good times.*

If only we'd taken a picture each year, you'd see the story of our lives in a single flipbook—youthful faces giving way to graying beards. Some faces changed. Some moved away. And some disappeared forever. This year, for the first time, we didn't see David Carson's 'PIG OUT' license plate among the parked cars. For forty years, we've eaten, laughed, and lived side-by-side. But time has a way of rearranging the table.

This year will mark our fortieth and final Pig Out Weekend. Who knew a stack of frozen steaks would lead to forty years of memories? Everyone wants to know why this tradition is ending. The truth is, we're old; and while this is an end of an era, these friendships will outlast any ending. I'm old enough now to not take any day for granted. The older you get, the quicker life and true friendships appreciate in value. As for me, I'll carry these memories like a belly full of king crab legs, stuffed to the brim, but worth every bite. And though we won't have our official Pig Out gathering, we'll always find time to connect. That's what true friends do best—get older, repeat the same stories, and laugh like we've never heard them.

AFTERWORD
BY ANNA HENKENS SCHMIDT

No form of entertainment is older than the story. From The Epic of Gilgamesh (circa 2100 BC) to the visual narratives etched on ancient cave walls, stories set us apart from the beasts, lend us glimpses of the Divine, and help us make sense of the world.

I had two distinct thoughts as I helped Donald craft this book of stories: Wow—what an interesting life. And then, Wow—we all live such interesting lives.

No one can deny Donald is a natural born storyteller. Not everyone can tell a tale about jumping over a dead body while out on a run or mistaking Roger Ebert's funeral procession as his own. That is uniquely Donald. Thankfully. But I do believe we are all storytellers, and we are all meant to share our stories.

Many Native American cultures passed on their stories through dancing. Shakespeare told stories through live adaptations on the stage. Mozart's "Requiem in D minor" set the universal experience of grief and hope to music. Our mom crafted narratives in her kitchen, passing down recipes for homemade bread, peanut brittle, and roasted turkey. Stories are all around us, if only we know to look for them.

Stories don't need to have a wild twist or a punch line to be meaningful. We can find stories in a donkey measuring tape (ask our sister Theresa about this one) or a dilapidated stuffed animal.

As Donald and I worked on this project, I kept returning to one idea: stories can't be owned. Sure, the stories in this book are from Donald's catalog of life experiences, but once shared, the stories become a part of the reader. As I listened to his reflections on the past and filtered them through my own words, the stories also became mine. And now that you've read these stories, they also belong to you.

If you take away anything from this book, I hope it's this: Pay the twenty-five cents to the strange man on the bus. Assume the snakes in front of Kenny's house are fake. And most of all, embrace your inner storyteller.

Even if your stories never leave the pig-out party, someone needs to hear them.

ACKNOWLEDGMENTS

It's been said that the last-born child in a family is the most perfect because the parents finally got it right. This is undeniably true of my little sister and coauthor Annie—who absolutely did not ghostwrite this acknowledgments section. She's certainly the bright light of my existence, the wind beneath my wings, and the reason I didn't give up halfway through the fourth story.

(Should I let Donald read this section before publication? Nah—let him be surprised.)

In all seriousness, we owe a great debt of gratitude to more people than could ever fit onto an acknowledgments page, though many of their names appear in these stories. We'd like to give special thanks to our beta readers who saved us from embarrassing misspellings and awkward sentence structures. Donna, Kerwin, Megan and Trevor; it's a big ask to read someone's unedited manuscript. Honestly, now you know how poor Kirk Fitcher must have felt when

Donald turned up naked in his hotel room. You've seen us at our worst, and you still gave us support and encouragement.

Thanks to Brianna, our niece and editor, for keeping us on track with your red pen—we prefer yours over Sister Monica's any day. You somehow managed to make sense of our chaos. No doubt you became an expert in cutting words back when Annie forced you to cut Grandma's lawn with scissors.

And to you—the reader—thank you for spending your time with us. As we said in the afterword, this story belongs to you now. If it meant something to you—or even just made you laugh in that "extolling parental wisdom through the Dollar Store" kind of way—we'd be grateful if you'd consider leaving a review. Reviews aren't just to feed our affirmation addiction; they're what help independent books like this one get discovered by others who might need the story just as much as you did.

To keep abreast of future projects, please consider signing up for our newsletter at **www.annahenkensschmidt.com.**

www.ingramcontent.com/pod-product-compliance
Lightning Source LLC
Chambersburg PA
CBHW070533310726
48976CB00002BA/619